AFTERLIFE

AFTERLIFE

Reports from the Threshold of Death

(Originally published under the title "The Waiting World")

ARCHIE MATSON

Harper & Row, Publishers

New York, Hagerstown, San Francisco, London

First Harper & Row paperback edition published in 1977.
This book was originally published under the title of The Waiting World.

ISBN 0-06-065465-1

LIBRARY OF CONGRESS CATALOG CARD NUMBER: 75-9338

77   78   79   80   10   9   8   7   6   5   4   3   2   1

To Our Grandson
TOM MATSON
1951-1975
The First of His Generation to Explore
THE WAITING WORLD
And to His Grandmother, My Beloved Wife
MARTHA WAGNER MATSON
1897-1975
Who Followed Him Seven Weeks Later.

Contents

Introduction

Death and its aftermath is the theme of this volume without apology or equivocation. It is the conviction of the writer that no question is ultimately more important — even when it comes to settling our urgent social and political problems such as war and crime. When it is generally recognised what real evidence about life after death is available, every thoughtful person will want to consider it.

The most explicit statement of "one world at a time" comes not from the pen of a modern philosopher or journalist, but from the lips of the Preacher in Ecclesiastes 9:3-6:

"This is an evil in all that is done under the sun, that one fate comes to all; also the hearts of men are full of evil, and madness is in their hearts while they live, and after that they are dead. But he who is joined with all the living has hope, for a living dog is better than a dead lion. For the living know that they will die, but the dead know nothing, and they have no more reward; but the memory of them is lost. Their love and their hate and their envy have already perished, and they have no more share in all that is under the sun."

Although few would state it so baldly, this is the actual philosophy of many in the modern world. It is the assumption back of "Eat, drink, and be merry, for tomorrow you die"; and "Get yours while the getting is good, and the devil take the hindmost." Our liberal church programs of country club entertainment on one side, and social reform on the other, often reflect the same empty faith. As much could be said of the violence in our country today. The so-called hippie and charismatic movements may both be in part revolts against the current materialism of "the establishment".

2

"One world at a time" is not the only answer to the question about what happens after death, as I used to think. Once I was blind. My faith was second-hand. My lips spoke without any real conviction but with only a faint hope. I wished there might be a heaven, but it seemed the dice were loaded against it.

But God still opens blind eyes! Some thirty years ago a greatly trusted friend told me of a personal experience similar to those in the next chapter. I still remember the ecstatic thrill that went through me — my wild surprise and my first surmise that faith could be fact! It was only a glimpse, a tiny beginning, a ray of promise; but I have never forgotten.

Later there came another shaft of light. I was alone out in the garden doing a chore of some kind when a question came into my mind: if God is God would He not be the same whether in the physics laboratory or the heart of a man? I still feel the answer: "Spiritual law can and must be parallel to physical law. *There can be no conflict between them.*" I still remember the glory of that moment. My heart beat faster as I caught the scent of something that had eluded me through the years, a secret known to saints and seers, the meaning of existence glimpsed by prophets and sensed by mystics.

So I became a hound on the trail of the meaning of heaven as the goal of earth. Although involved in the details of parish administration and weekly sermons, I sniffed every breeze, always hoping to get wind of another world. I listened to the stories people told, read the books they wrote, but most of them left me like the blind man who saw men "as trees, walking" (Mark 8:22-25) after Jesus had touched him just once. The scientific skeptic that I am would not, perhaps could not, see. I believed with my fingers crossed, which meant that I was not at all sure. My dreams were like those of the maiden: "He loves me, he loves me not."

Sometimes it would seem to me that nothing happened at death except death, and I would wonder — why worry about the war, or traffic fatalities, or high blood pressure? We must each die at some time or other, and that is that! *If nothing happens after death, then nothing really matters before death,* as long as we are comfortable, fairly secure, and not too deeply involved with people. The only sensible logic would be suicide whenever pain exceeded pleasure; and in the meantime to eat, drink, and be merry — and forget the dying.

Then again I would argue with myself: suppose there is a waiting world? Can't we be sure of it without having to die first in order to find out? I did find some answers in books, although many were dreary and repetitious. Other were exciting, but as unbelievable as science fiction — as I thought then. Yet once in a while one would set the bells ringing in my heart, and I would hear the faint beat of another Drummer.

Besides books there were people, and flesh and blood proved more convincing than printer's ink, though the great majority of those with whom I talked were either searching as I was, or had given it up as a bad job. Now and then, however, I would find one who carried an aura of sure knowledge that was contagious. With some it was the certainty of experience, and with others the assurance of faith, but in either case their lives and faces told me all doubt and fear were gone. As they spoke there would be a light in the eyes, a catch in the voice, and I knew they were telling a true story still hidden from my heart. Some of their reports, moreover, could be checked, and rather gingerly I began to step out where they had walked and confirm what they had learned. A sense of certainty slowly became mine as I tested and confirmed what they claimed to have experienced. There is a spiritual world both here and hereafter, and we can be sure of if now.

Once a man experiences a thing himself there can be no more of doubting. He knows! Whether it be Fiji, a new baby in the home, or the touch of God — it is his knowledge, and he can give his testimony. So it was with me. And, being the person I am, I put it into a book (now out of print), *Mystery to Meaning,* seeking to pass on my discovery of the reality behind human experience.

And now, fifteen years or so later, I am driven to make a further witness, not about our earthly lives, but about the life that comes after this one, the waiting world, and the advance information available about it. Just as knowledge of the physical world and how to control it has been skyrocketing for a hundred years, so also has evidence of the reality and nature of the next world. The latter fact is not so well known, lost in the welter of cars, planes and TV, not to mention the atom, still uncontrolled, and the moon we are beginning to explore. It is this evidence we will be outlining and evaluating in this volume.

3

When put together, the data now available is as credible as much that is accepted day after day in our courts. It is as reliable as most of the articles in our magazines and newspapers; as valid as the bases for our daily judicial decisions and legislative action. After carefully examining the pertinent phenomena and comparing reports from many sources, I am convinced that most of them agree in essence and corroborate each other. In every case where I have checked them or been able to repeat the experiments, the result has been to strengthen the evidence and my own faith in it. Thus I have become both reporter and witness, each confirming and amplifying the other. As a witness I can testify to the nature and apparent validity of the evidence; and, as a researcher and reporter, confirm the emotional depth and intellectual breadth and consistency of the reports of life beyond death. Here indeed is glorious fulfilment of the best that heart and mind can picture, in ever-broadening vistas. All this, and more, awaits us as fast and as far as we are willing and ready to accept it.

I am also trying to be scientific in considering and following the canons of logical thinking and research which have remade the modern world. Moreover, in atomic physics and recent biological research there are pointers toward larger aspects of reality beyond the physical. Here are the crucial questions of human destiny, questions as taboo to the scientific materialist as eating pork to an orthodox Jew or mixed nude bathing to most Americans.

Although this volume is not religious or devotional in tone, it does take the primary sources of Christianity, the life and teachings of Jesus and Paul, and relate them as integral parts of our evidence. Using the methods of science, it attempts to lay a foundation for a faith that could revolutionize much modern thinking as well as the social order.

Religion and science are not two contradictory disciplines, but partners in the search for meaning both on the near and far sides of death, the great divider. There are those who believe that religion can only claim the allegiance of modern man when once again it can speak with authority about the world to come. It could be that *a rational approach to faith and a wider application of the methods of science to the whole of life would provide a basis for the recapture of trust and authority in both worlds.* This is the thesis of this book.

Behind science and religion are five types of phenomena which provide the primary source material and evidence for the answers to our questions. Yet they are commonly rejected by both disciplines and rarely discussed in conventional circles. We sweep them under the bed and trust that our friends will not get too inquisitive about them. Still, they have a way of coming out when fears are allayed and tongues loosed.

For example, the dying can sometimes peer over the wall and give us a bit of advance information. The dead do come back and report what they have found! Others tell what they are experiencing and how they have changed their minds. All together they confirm much of what Jesus of Nazareth and the Apostle Paul say in the New Testament, and then go further in describing a life glorious beyond anything man has ever dared to dream.

Why not give this array of witnesses a chance to be heard? If this seems too far out for rational consideration, read it as science fiction. There is always the possibility that it might be true — at least in part. It would be well to remember that many of the inventions and discoveries of the twentieth century were first envisaged by science-fiction writers. Thus Jules Verne a century ago described travel to the moon in rocket ships strikingly similar to those now being launched. The fiction of one day is often the truth of the next. The dream of today may well be the reality of tomorrow — or of the twenty-first century.

If exploration of this field seems a sacrilege to some, it

would be well to remember that Jesus talked with the dead (Luke 9:27-36). He said (John 8:32-38), "You will know the truth and the truth will make you free . . . If the Son makes you free, you will be free indeed." Perhaps we are now in a position to understand almost the last words he spoke to his disciples (John 16:12-15): "I have yet many things to say to you, but you cannot bear them now. When the spirit of truth comes, he will guide you into all the truth; . . . and he will declare to you the things that are to come."

4

One world at a time is not enough. A social and educational system that deals with life only from the cradle to the grave can provide neither the clarity of vision nor the qualities of character required for a maturing and enduring society. Two world wars in one generation and the current breakdown of law and order in our city streets and college campuses amply confirm this. A religion that deals only with this world cannot long hold the loyalty of men, nor inspire the disciplines required for an orderly society in an era of peace. On the other hand, a church that speaks primarily of "pie in the sky" will not be heeded by a generation obsessed by material comforts and physical thrills.

Man is a creature of two worlds: the world of the flesh with its pains and pleasures, marriage and children, work and play; and the world of the spirit with its fears and faith, its ideals and sacrifices, its promise of God and heaven. The church as a whole can command the allegiance of modern man only when it can once more speak with authority about the world to come, and then with integrity about the ills of this world.

Without faith in life beyond death man is merely an animal in spite of having the power to make of earth a hell — or a heaven. There can be no ultimate divorce in this life between flesh and spirit, between earth and heaven. To succeed on earth we must have a vision of heaven, not necessarily the heaven of angel choirs and golden streets, but one that can be tested and tasted now. The ethical drive for a new age on earth must come from a clear vision of the new world beyond earth waiting for each of us. Only thus can we pray with intelligence and sincerity, "Thy will be done on earth as it is in heaven."

So this is a marriage manual — the union of flesh and faith — claiming to confirm the reality of heaven by the logic and experience of earth. Incidentally, a lot of earthly marriages might be made worth extending even into the life beyond by introducing some heavenly virtues into everyday living and loving.

What happens at death? From the standpoint of earth it is the same as for all animals — whether quickly or slowly, peacefully or violently — the heart ceases to beat and the processes of decay set in. It is the same for all — rich and poor, Christian or otherwise, black or white — no matter how they try to postpone it through medicine, forget it by silence, bury it in busyness, or speed it by suicide.

What happens at death? Before we dismiss the question as too morbid to discuss, or too hopeless of answer to investigate, let us begin by looking at a few samples of the stories people tell when their fears and inhibitions are laid aside.

Part one

GLIMPSES OF ETERNITY

1 Stories People Tell

"What are you writing about?"

This is the question I fish for and manage to get quite frequently as I talk with people wherever I find them alone, at dinner, on a plane, after a meeting, in their homes. In reply I give briefly the idea of this book, and then begin to tell stories — tall tales it often seems to them — of my own experiences and those of others. When they begin to get fidgety and only half listen I quickly change the subject. But again and again I recognize a glint in the eye and know a story is coming.

There have been scores of these in recent years, personal experiences of ordinary people and their families. Often they are told eagerly, as for the first time the speakers know they will not be thought crazy. A sympathetic ear and the assurance that others have similar experiences are better than wine for loosening the tongue. Here are a few incidents of varied type that have come to my ears. Others will be found scattered throughout the book. These are not the most dramatic ones, but are more typical of those that seem to be locked up in the memories of a great many people.

I was telling stories one day to a woman I have known for half a century, a college graduate at nineteen, a beloved grandmother, and a leader both in her church and in her social circles.

Finally she spoke. "You know, Archie, I had a strange experience many years ago. I have never dared tell it to a living soul for fear people would think I had gone off the deep end. I was very sick after surgery when I found myself floating over the head of the bed and looking down on my body. Then I found myself back in my body, but I have no idea how I got there."

I asked for more specific details and if there was any connection between her body on the bed and her body floating face down above it, but she could recall nothing except the one vivid picture. She was eighty-eight at the time and for possibly fifty years had repressed the whole matter in the fear that people would think she was losing her mind.

How much needless worry she had suffered! If she had known how common such experiences are, her own could well have demonstrated to her that she was not born to die with her body. Yet she did have one other outstanding extra sensory perception experience involving other members of her family. When I reminded her of it she could remember nothing although her mind is keen on most subjects.

Her sister-in-law told me of the near death of her own father who later reported that he was greeted by his wife, Mary, and their little daughter, Emma, who had died when she was four. They told him it was not quite time for him to join them, but they would be waiting for him. He recovered and lived for a number of years always with the certainty that his beloved Mary and precious little Emma were very much alive and eager to welcome him. When he finally did die, those at his bedside reported that his face became radiant as he slipped away, apparently seeing something which was invisible to them.

When I went back to check on the story my friend denied ever having told it, and said I must be thinking of somebody else. I did not argue the matter, and only tell it here as illustrative of the great amount of hidden and repressed evidence for life apart from the physical body. In two cases in one family, each unbeknown to the other, I was able to get a fleeting glimpse of something akin to family skeletons never to be exposed to public view, and usually forgotten, or at least denied.

In a high school Spanish class the lesson dealt with a character who experienced visions and dreams. The teacher told of his *drowning* in Lake Erie.

"I had been moonlighting as a guard at a private beach and

decided to take a swim before going home. The next thing I knew, I was surrounded by deep darkness and a feeling of sublime peace.

"As I moved apparently in slow motion through the darkness engulfing me as soft as velvet, I became aware of lights glowing from the edges of the darkness. The lights came closer . . . or I came closer to the lights . . . and I knew that they were shades of blues from aqua to deepest navy and greens from new yellow greens to deepest hunter green.

"Floating through these softly swirling colors I heard music. I only knew it was music and could not distinguish it as either vocal or instrumental. All was peace. All was beautiful. All was painless.

"Then I was shot through these colors and melodies as from the mouth of a cannon. The pain was agonizing. I was receiving artificial respiration and returning to life."

I have before me as I write a letter from a doctor's widow recounting four experiences through which her eyes had been opened to reality. We had discussed them over the phone and she had agreed to put them into writing. Two of them dealt with somewhat ordinary out-of-the-body experiences twenty years apart, and another with the death of her husband. The fourth described the time she "nearly died" after the birth of her youngest child by Caesarean section. Here is her story:

"I was going down a long tunnel, white-tiled like the old Illinois Central tunnels to the trains at Chicago. I was being propelled forward, but I had no money, no ticket, and could not remember who I was or where I was to go. The tunnel was wide and light and there were many people around . . . I was beginning to panic when I remembered the name Jesus, and at once knew who I was; I had a ticket and whatever I needed for money, and I knew my destination. Then I came back on rolling waves of the hymn 'Jesus, Lover of My Soul'. My feet and legs were utterly cold, and from the attitudes of the obstetrician and anesthetist, as well as the nurses, I *must* have been nearly dead."

Recently my wife and I were guests in a home in Santa Ana, California, when a neighbour dropped in. The husband is a newspaper reporter and his wife Mary has been a teacher. Both of them are well-balanced and used to sifting evidence before speaking. The talk shifted as usual to my writing. Finally Mary told us about her mother's death. I asked her to write it to make sure I had it correctly. Here is a portion of what she wrote.

"Mother and I were very close. We were not only mother and daughter, but very good friends. As she was entering the final stages of her bout with cancer I spent a whole night with her at the hospital.

"No sooner did I reach home when I was called on the phone and urged to come immediately with my father and sister. Mother gave us a smile of recognition and closed her eyes. I had such a strong feeling that she was well again that I spoke it out loud.

"The nurse tried to usher us out of the room. My father and sister left, but I stayed. The doctor then ordered me to leave. I had tossed my purse on a cot across the room, and started to get it when I had another strong feeling that would not be denied. I turned and looked at Mother. Her face was serene, and floating from her and above her toward the ceiling was a bright, golden, shapeless mist — heavier in some places than in others.

"For a minute I held my breath — then, needing confirmation, I asked the doctor if he could see the same thing. He answered that he could, but that it was not unusual, and that it was 'gas escaping from the body'.

"I know that this was a message from Mother. Nothing about it was frightening, all was good, and I knew without a doubt that Mother was well and perfect again, and that I would not fear death when it came to me."

Dr Robert Crookall has collected about a dozen similar incidents.[1] Many others are given by DeWitt Miller.[2] Some of the terms used to describe the emanation are a white hazy mist, a violet cloud, a dim misty cloud, and a smoke-like vapor, but in no case other than this have I found any suggestion that it was "a gas escaping from the body".

One summer night my wife and I gave a small dinner party. The talk was gay as I had married one of the couples not long before. After the meal I found myself in a corner with the head of a large manufacturing company. The talk quickly drifted to my writing and the stories I hear. He recalled the death of his mother several years before. She had had a very severe heart attack, but through modern medical techniques was finally brought back to fair health. However, she was a very different person as she was now aware of two worlds: the present physical life with its problems and pains, and the goodness and joy of the world to come. She awaited eagerly her time to go. Strangely enough she was not able to pass on this assurance to her sons, both of whom I know well, but her surviving sister at ninety-three has accepted it and so looks forward expectantly for her own time to move on.

In the summer of 1966 we were guests in a home near Vancouver, British Columbia. Our host and hostess had just received word that their only son Philip had been lost at sea in a shipwreck off the coast of Australia. Their state of shock can well be imagined. As we ate lunch I was using every means at my disposal to make real the viewpoint I am developing in this book, that the life beyond is as sure and real as anything we know in the physical world. Only later did the mother explain what happened as I was talking. As I spoke there appeared on the wall facing her what she described as a life-sized picture of Philip in perfect health and smiling at her. This they accepted as his confirmation of the truth of what I was saying. Philip wanted his parents to know that all was well with him, and that they should continue to live and rejoice in that fact.

I have in front of me a letter dated 20 September 1968 from my friend Anna, a woman of great spiritual and intellectual depth and leadership in southern California. After explaining that 7 November 1950 was their daughter's fourteenth birthday and that her (Anna's) mother was coming over to help in the celebration, she went on:

"Shortly after one o'clock the telephone rang. It was a nurse in a doctor's office calling to tell me that my mother had been seriously hurt, and to rush over to Whittier as quickly as I could. I hurried to get a few things together and then stepped into the shower for a hasty refresher. As I was standing under the water, I suddenly felt completely enfolded in love and light; and had my outer ear registered it, nothing could have been more clear than my mother saying, "Everything is all right, Anna."

"As I was speeding over to Whittier, I suddenly felt that she was sitting beside me. I was thinking ruefully about a time shortly before when I had been rather thoughtless and inconsiderate, and then my mind began to pick up other times when I wished I had not said this or done that. Again, it was as clear as though she had spoken aloud, 'Don't let any of those things bother you, Anna. I understand them all.' And never again has the thought of them worried me.

"I had this feeling of her being right there on the seat beside me for several miles, and then at a certain intersection as 'we' entered Whittier, I felt that she left. Then I began to remember all the things that had been said down through the years that were to prepare me for this moment. A few months before her passing Mother told me of a dream she had of being all alone on a very lonely road, and in her fright calling out to her children but none of them heard her; and then she looked up and saw Papa, who had gone on about ten years previously, coming down the road with open arms to greet her.

"When I reached my destination I was greeted by my cousin and her minister, who told me my mother had met with an accident and had died about twenty minutes before. As I figured, this would have been just as I was standing under the shower, and had the wonderful feeling of being surrounded with love and light. To my astonishment I felt not sorrow at my loss, but only joy at her reunion with her loved ones."

All of these are but garden variety examples of the accounts to which I have listened in recent years. I have deliberately chosen them because the more spectacular stories often bring doubt and incredulity, creating a barrier, while the more common incidents draw people together and bring out similar and often half-forgotten experiences. I have come to think of these as part of the unspoken and hidden drama which should be recognized and accepted as our human heritage just as much as birth and education or politics, and available to all.

But now let me tell another much more dramatic story. I have chosen not to use the full names of the people involved so far, but the persons in the following story are well known, and it has often been publicly told and tape-recorded. Moreover, the medical aspects can be checked against hospital records, so I will use their full names.

There were three of us, beside our hostess, one day in 1959 in a home in Burbank, California. One was Dr E. Stanley Jones, a missionary and evangelist; another was Mrs Louise Eggleston, a lecturer and retreat leader. I was the third, largely a silent listener. The conversation was scintillating, but I have forgotten almost everything that was said except for one story. It was told by Mrs Eggleston about the *two deaths* of her husband, Aubrey, who was a leading banker for many years in Norfolk, Virginia. She has corrected and approved the story which I quote in her own words.

"One afternoon some twenty-five years ago my husband came home from the bank a little early and said he had a spell of indigestion, and would go out and play a round of golf to work it off. It was worse when he returned a couple of hours later, but he said he would try again by going bowling with our son Laddie. So off they went. About ten p.m. they came in, Aubrey obviously in great pain and looking ghastly . . . He said he would have to give in and that I could call a doctor. Aubrey was the kind of man who was never sick and never went to a doctor so while he went to bed I called a personal friend on the Church Official Board who happened also to be a heart specialist.

"By the time the doctor arrived Aubrey was practically unconscious. After listening carefully with his stethoscope the doctor turned to me and said, 'I'm sorry, Mrs Eggleston, but it is too late. There is nothing that can be done. Your husband will be gone within half an hour.'

" 'You mean, Doctor,' I said, 'that there is nothing that can be done medically to save my husband's life?'

" 'Yes, absolutely nothing.' (Remember that this was back

in the early thirties and that there have been many advances in handling heart attacks since then.)

" 'Well,' I said, 'if you have done all that you can, I'll do what I can.'

" 'But you don't understand, Mrs Eggleston. It is too late. There is absolutely nothing that can save him now. The main artery supplying blood to one side of his heart has burst. His heart is already gone for all intents and purposes. But I will remain with you until it is over. It can't be more than half an hour, and you would have to call me to come right back.'

"I went into the next room and phoned my prayer partner, explaining the situation and asking her to pray in her home as I would in mine, knowing that Jesus healed every soul who came to him in any need, and giving thanks and visualizing my husband's perfect healing. We would continue thus to pray until we were given His peace.

"One full hour passed before I felt that inner peace and knew that all was well. No sound had come from the next room and when I went in the doctor was sound asleep. I am confident that the Lord had to put him to sleep while He healed the patient. In order not to embarrass the doctor I called in and asked how my husband was coming along. You can imagine how chagrined the doctor was. He was even more surprised when he discovered Aubrey was not only alive, but his heartbeat was much stronger. He simply could not understand how this could be.

"Well, to make a long story short, Aubrey was completely restored in a matter of two weeks or so, and lived for eighteen years more, the most active and useful of his entire life. He even took part in state golf tournaments, and worked long hours especially during the war when we were short of help, heading up the Norfolk area war loan drives, and carrying his full load in all church work.

"But he was not the same man. He had died and gone into the next life where he was met by many of his loved ones who had passed over before him. He now knew from personal experience the wonder and glory of heaven. Always he had been a Christian and a loyal member of the church, active especially in its business affairs. However, he would never go to a funeral or take part in any discussion of death. These simply were not for him because of several tragic experiences with death in his boyhood. But now he knew the truth and had lost all fear. All during the war there was nobody in Norfolk in such demand to talk with parents who had lost their sons. He could bring real comfort because he knew what their boys were facing in the next life. He had been there.

"So it was for eighteen years. Then he realized that it was his time to go. Laddie had been killed when a plane exploded in 1949, and Aubrey wanted to join his son in heaven. So he arranged his affairs and had his successor trained and appointed to take his place in the bank. Then he went with him to a meeting of the American Bankers Association in Detroit while I was leader in a healing camp in Pennsylvania. I came back just in time to drive out and pick them up at the airport, but instead, received an urgent message to come at once as Aubrey was in a Detroit hospital.

"I got on a plane that night but it was five the next morning when I reached the hospital. As soon as my husband saw me he lay back in bed perfectly satisfied, and went into a light coma. The next hours were some of the strangest and most wonderful of my life. Aubrey was in two worlds at the same time. He was not only aware of me and talking to me, but he greeted by name some thirty or forty friends and relatives who were waiting for him. The last one was John Moreland, the poet, who had been best man at our wedding, and who had died unbeknown to him just two weeks before. It was a happy reunion!

"As he greeted each one on the other side his face took on a greater glow of spiritual radiance. I watched his breath get shorter and shorter, knowing that he was slowly 'passing over', but never once even considered calling for help. I knew it was intended for me to see his happy entrance into the great beyond. When he was gone I called the doctor.

"After pronouncing him dead the doctor asked if they could perform an autopsy as my husband had just come in the night before and they had not been able to make a clear diagnosis. I agreed and said I would wait. About noon he came back to me and said, 'Mrs Eggleston, did you say that your husband had been active recently? We found that one side of his heart was like leather, and we do not see how he could have been more than a wheel chair invalid, if he could live at all.'

"I let the doctor know that the last eighteen years were the most active and productive of his life, and asked for extra copies of the autopsy report, one for the doctor who had watched his first death and recovery eighteen years before, and who still could not understand how my husband could be active and well; and another for the Norfolk hospital records where it is still available for any doctor who wants to check on it."

These are but samples of the scores of narratives from the people involved, and of the hundreds that have come to me second-hand or from printed sources. Some of these will be discussed in later chapters, but here is a condensation from the many to be found in magazines.

"Mrs Mary Grohe, 50, of Stowe, Ohio, recently returned from clinical death to relate an amazing experience. The story was reported in the *Akron Beacon Journal* by staff writer Judie Craig.

"Mrs Grohe, who suffers from a heart condition, was in Lakeside Hospital to replace her pacemaker with a new one. Two days after the operation she had a heart attack. A nurse arrived just as she fell dead on the floor, and began a resuscitation process which doctors completed less than three minutes later. An electrical shock applied to the patient's heart brought her back to life.

"She related that while clinically dead she seemed to be hurtling like a projectile through space that was alternately red and black. At the same time she was aware of the word 'death'.

"Then, Mrs Grohe said she saw her mother who had died in 1949. Held in her mother's right arm was Mrs Grohe's baby who was stillborn in 1941. Then her mother put out her left hand in a gesture and said, 'Not yet, Mary.' "

The figure then faded from view, Mrs Grohe concluded, and she saw her own body on the hospital floor with the doctors working over it.[3]

That these previews of the waiting world are far more common than usually realized is suggested by what happened to William D. Pelley, the rebel son of a Methodist minister and a radical novelist and editor. He wrote in the March 1929 issue of the *American Magazine* about two mystical experiences by which his whole life was transformed. The article brought some 20,000 replies, of which less than two dozen were unfavourable, and most of which recounted similar incidents. This would seem to confirm my own feeling that great numbers of people have stories to tell of the life beyond death whenever their fears are broken down and they have a sympathetic listener or reader.

These memories that people hold in their hearts but hesitate to share because of conventional taboos differ very much from the commonly accepted scientific concepts of life and death. The usual medical viewpoint is that they are hallucinations. Orthodox science ignores them as being delusions because nothing can be real which cannot be weighed or measured, including the non-physical aspects of death. To a large extent this has also been the practical conclusions of better educated church members, as well as their theological leaders.

On the other hand, the more traditional and conservative churches have usually disregarded such reports while preaching the heaven described in the book of Revelation and a hell of everlasting fire. Both of these viewpoints are inconsistent with much in the Bible and the experiences of many of their members are usually silenced by the spirit of scepticism which has dominated the twentieth century so far.

As a result of this conspiracy of silence only a small number of people are prepared to think realistically about either their own deaths or those of their families. Small wonder that the psychologist Fritz Kunkel told an audience of Protestant ministers that their biggest failure was in not adequately preparing their people for death and bereavement.

So, it may be helpful for some to examine the scientific and religious theories about death before examining the evidence for the waiting world. This I will try to do in Part II of this book. References to the Four Watchmen of Science are explained in Chapter II.

2 What the Dying Tell Us

We come now to deathbed experiences the first of our five sources of direct information about the next world. The story of Aubrey Eggleston's death just told is a good introduction. Many reports of similar experiences would indicate that we do not have to wait for death to get a preview of what is in store for us. In some cases we apparently look over the wall or through a window and see for ourselves. In others, our friends in that land come to meet us. Folklore from all centuries is full of these stories, but there would be little reason to take them seriously in spite of their strange consistency if new examples did not continue to show themselves. The most familiar ancient story is the one about Stephen just before he died by stoning as recorded in Acts 7:54-9.

> Now when they heard these things they were enraged, and they ground their teeth against him. But he [Stephen] full of the Holy Spirit, gazed into heaven and . . . said, "Behold, I see the heavens opened, and the Son of man standing at the right hand of God." But they cried out with a loud voice and stopped their ears and rushed upon him. Then they cast him out of the city and stoned him. . . . And as they were stoning Stephen he prayed, "Lord Jesus, receive my spirit."

Most people probably feel that this is a biblical story which has no relevance today, and therefore really tells us nothing. What actually happened to Stephen is uncertain, except that it was so vivid and alluring to him that the prospect of an immediate and painful death held no terror. It has been claimed that it was hallucination brought on by hysteria. Standing by itself that could well be, but here is another tale, the most recent I have heard.

"The night before this is being written, my wife and I were dinner guests in a home across the street. The talk turned to writing as our hostess is the author of many books, and I said I was starting this chapter on deathbed visions. Then she recalled visiting her parents' home in Johnson City, Kansas, as a young woman when her grandmother lay dying. It seemed to the family that their beloved was gone, but she roused up and appeared quite put out because she was still in this life. She had already seen over the wall and described it like a park more lovely than anything she had ever seen or imagined. She also told them of music like a great symphony of voices more lovely than earth could give. After this, what a letdown to open her eyes and see her family hovering over her as she lay on her bed in extreme weariness and weakness! She had both seen and heard the glory waiting and was most eager to return and explore it. Her experience did not include any other persons as far as my friend remembers except that the music was a chorus of voices. This only means that her awareness began with the country beyond, while that of others begins with people who have preceded them in death. It illustrates again the fact that each person is different and has his or her own set of experiences going into the New World. Yet they all fit into certain categories, depending on the person involved, the manner of death, and the situation at the time."

More common are incidents like the following told by Harold Paul Sloan over a Philadelphia radio station in the spring of 1943.[1] The secretary and the daughter of Dr Johnston had told the whole of the following story to Dr Sloan while it was still fresh in their minds.

"Dr Leonard Johnston was a distinguished Philadelphia physician who passed to the other world about a decade ago. He became ill one day and lay down on a couch in his office. His wife and his secretary were with him. Suddenly he called their attention to 'most noble' music which they could not hear.

"Then he seemed to see his brother Joe (who had died twenty-five years before) and remarked, 'There's Joe, but he does not speak to me.' He called to him and asked why he didn't speak, and then said how fine he looked. Then Joe must have replied, for he said, 'Hello, Joe,' with an evident thrill of pleasure. A little later Dr Johnston's father and mother must have come into the room for he addressed each of them.

"Later the Savior appeared and called him. He described it to his secretary, 'Look, Mildred, He reached out his hand to me like this,' and raised his arm. And then he added, 'It would not be right to try to live now when Jesus Himself has called me.' "

Music is so commonly reported by the dying that a whole book could be written about it. Elizabeth Yates, in the August 1967 *Guideposts,* wrote of a grocer friend, Mr B., who described his wife's death the night before.

"It was so beautiful," he repeated. "I was sitting beside her bed last evening when she turned to me and said, 'Can you hear it?' 'Hear what?' I asked. 'The music,' she said, 'The music. Listen!' Her face was aglow, her eyes were shining and she raised her head from the pillow as if to hear it better.

"I listened, but that music was not for me. I knew by the light in her face what joy it was giving her, and when her head slipped back on the pillow I would not have done anything to keep her from hearing that glorious music forever."[2]

Dr Sloan has a similar story about two-year-old Florence Repp as she lay dying in her grandmother's arms. Suddenly she exclaimed, "Mommom, moosic! Moosic! Don't you hear the moosic?" "No, dear, I don't hear any music," replied the grandmother, but the girl didn't want to miss hearing it. "Shush, Mommom, moosic! They're playing up there," she said as she pointed upward. She died almost instantly.

There are many incidents of a similar nature involving small children, for example, two-year-old Robin, the mongoloid daughter of Roy Rogers and Dale Evans, here related by her nurse to Dale on the day of the funeral.

"Almost all day Sunday Robin was unconscious, her eyes closed. Well, just a few seconds before she died, she opened her eyes real wide. Then she lifted both her little hands toward the ceiling and smiled radiantly, just as if she knew where she was going and was glad." The nurse hesitated. "I've heard of such things happening, Dale, but in all my years of nursing this is the first time I've ever seen it. And I am sure your baby met our Lord. *I saw it happen.*"[3]

Readers may remember how the twelve-year-old mother-less Lowell Jones,[4] after he had lost the power of speech at the end of his short life, "raised his hands in wonder and got enough voice to say, 'Oh, Mother,' as though they had found each other in the world that is Real."

A more recent report[5] by the Washington correspondent, Ruth Montgomery, quotes the mother of a six-week-old boy with a defective heart: "Suddenly our little baby, who was lying in his crib, sat up all by himself and looked straight at me. I was terribly shaken, not only because I had never heard of so young a baby raising and holding himself erect, but because of the unfathomable look in his big blue eyes. It was an other-world gaze, wise and adult, which plainly told me that he was not going to live, and that I was not to grieve."

Hundreds of these stories have been collected. Almost all concur on the glories which open up to the dying while they are still on this side of the grave and are able to communicate to those by their bedsides. Many of them describe a path by a brook among indescribable flowers and trees, but even more indicate the presence of friends or relatives who have previously died.[6]

The most detailed study[7] in this field is by Dr Karlis Osis, Research Director of the Parapsychology Foundation of New York, who sent a questionnaire to 10,000 doctors and nurses chosen at random throughout the country. They were asked to state how many deaths they had witnessed, and the proportion of those who were conscious through the last hours. Then they were asked about the emotional attitudes of the latter, and any special experiences they seemed to have, such as visions or hallucinations, which might relate to their feelings.

Such random questionnaires usually bring very little response, but in this case 640 were returned, about three times as many as Dr Osis had expected. These came from 285 doctors and 355 nurses who estimated that they had witnessed some 35,000 deaths of which about one in ten, or 3,500, were conscious up to the last hours. These figures were far different from what they would have been a century ago because, as one correspondent caustically remarked, "Nowadays man dies doped." Whenever possible replies were followed up by additional correspondence and telephone calls to get more detailed information.

Throughout his monograph Dr Osis correctly uses the word 'hallucination' to describe the experiences of the dying because the primary dictionary meaning of the word is "an apparent perception, as by sight or hearing, for which there is no physical external cause". However, I will use the term 'vision' because in the minds of most people 'hallucination' means "suffering from illusion or false notions", which is its secondary meaning. Because a dying person claims to hear voices or music, or to see things beyond my power to sense, does not mean that he is deluded or suffering from a false notion. My wife is aware of odors that mean nothing to me, but I can read from a Greek Testament which is Greek to her. Better yet, I watch the face of a man with receivers clamped to his ears and realize that he is following the progress of a World Series baseball game a thousand miles away. So I shall write of the 'experiences' and 'visions' of the dying. They may well be just as real to them as radio or television, but calling them 'hallucinations' would make them seem false to many readers.

But first let us notice the mood of dying persons. The most common attitudes toward death are panic, anxiety and fear. We speak of a situation as "desperate" or "hopeless" when we mean that death is impending, but both doctors and nurses in their replies to Dr Osis agreed "that fear is not the dominant emotion in dying patients". Even more surprising was "the large number who are said to be elated at the hour of death. This mood is apparently quite frequent among terminal patients. This was confirmed by 169 doctors and nurses reporting 753 cases where they observed a sudden rise of mood to exaltation in dying patients."

This mood is confirmed by the incidental comments made by those reporting, such as references to the "peace that occurs in spite of the pain and discomfort previously seen" and "the extreme strength just before death". Several examples of this in dying children have already been mentioned. One doctor wrote how these observations had changed his own philosophy: "There is such a resigned, peaceful, almost happy expression which comes over the patient. It is hard to explain but it leaves me with the feeling that I would not be afraid to die."

While some of those responding tried to explain these experiences as a result of a lack of blood supply to the brain and thus being out of touch with reality, others wrote of religious beliefs and practices as being involved, or, as one letter expressed it, "the eyes of the patient open wide staring at something very surprising, reaching out". What did they see or hear? The answer to this question forms the main body of Dr Osis' monograph and our chief concern in this chapter.

When the questionnaires and follow-up queries for details had been analyzed, Dr Osis and his colleagues found they had 753 cases of visions of non-human content, largely in accord with traditional religious concepts or of scenes of great beauty and often with brilliant colors. In addition there were 1,370 who reported seeing one or more spirits. This is a very high percentage of the 3,500 or so cases of those conscious up to the last, even though it may include some who lapsed into unconsciousness later, or persons who may have been counted twice because both persons and scenery were involved. This would suggest that those who are conscious up to the moment of death are very likely to have out-of-this-world visions or experiences which may be observed or reported at the time. The experiences of those who come close to death but later recover, which will be discussed in the next chapter, indicates that many more may well have these experiences but are unable to communicate them.

The large number of cases reported in this project were of patients whose mentality was not disturbed by sedatives, other medication, or high body temperature. "The emotional quality of the visionary experience is expressed predominantly as indescribable beauty and peace. There were only two cases in the whole collection which struck a distressing emotional note, a small minority indeed compared to the beauty, joy and elation usually reported."

The final conclusions of the research program were to confirm previous studies and much popular belief that terminal patients often have visions of dead persons who claim to welcome and aid the patient's transition to the next life.

What shall we do with these stories? They come from the

dying of all ages, centuries and races. Not only saints and religious people, but often those who are not expecially pious, such as Thomas Edison, are reported to have seen the beauty of another world as they were dying. Can all of these be only delusions, the strange hallucination of death, as orthodox medical opinion often puts it?

Strangely enough, these visions do not come to the very evil — or is it strange? Perhaps this is just what we should expect. But that is not the subject of this book. However, anybody who is reading this need have nothing to fear about death, judging from the numbers and kinds of those who have a preview of the life beyond.

Or could it be that all of this is delusion or wish-thinking? Standing alone these stories carry weight with those who want to believe, who are already convinced in their hearts. But that does not make them true. People have always been able to make themselves believe. Between 1937 and 1945 we saw a whole nation, one of the best educated and most scientific in Europe, follow after a delusion of race destiny which had little basis in fact, but which led to the most destructive war in all history. False visions lead to nightmares, and delusions to suicide. Deathbeds may presage not life but death — unless there is other evidence. But there is! Two kinds of it!

The first sort of evidence is from situations where others present see the same vision as the dying. This is not the same as seeing the spirit leave as a light-coloured cloud or vapor as described in Chapter I. Thus Gladys Osborne Leonard wrote[8] of being present at the death of her brother-in-law and seeing the form of a girl of about eighteen dressed in the clothing of the 1880s "bending over the body in a tender, expectant manner. Afterwards his relatives told me that it was his sister who died at the age of eighteen (more than fifty years before) . . . The breathing stopped quite suddenly and yet with absolute ease. There was no gasp or sign of the slightest discomfort; simply withdrawal."

The story told by Dr Harmon Bro, psychologist and Dean of Theology at Drake University, about a friend of his, a business executive who "glimpsed the smiling members of his family who had preceded him in death" is quite different.

"It happened when his elderly sister lay dying of cancer. She had remained rational to the end, despite her pain. Shortly before she stopped breathing her tired face lit up and, to the astonishment of her grieving family, she cried out with delight, 'Oh, yes.' Then with a broad smile and happy nods, her eyes wide, she greeted her father, mother, and brother who had preceded her in death. 'I'm coming,' she said as she died.

"Her brother was stunned. For he had seen what she saw just as she spoke. He never forgot the expressions on those hearty, well-loved faces that had caught his vision as his sister died; years later he could describe to me the look of each one."[9]

The second type is even more circumstantial. Although there are comparatively few reports of clear-minded dying persons having visions of living persons, there are many of persons seeing those whom they thought to be living, but who had died, and of their consequent surprise. I have collected twelve such stories and have reports of others. Let me quote just two of them.

One concerns the death of a sister of Natalie Kalmus, a Hollywood Technicolor expert. Miss Kalmus had promised that no drugs would be administered to ease her sister's last hours because she was not at all afraid to die and was convinced that death would be a beautiful experience. Miss Kalmus describes the final scene:

"I sat on her bed and took her hand. It was on fire. Then she seemed to rise up in bed almost to a sitting position.

" 'Natalie!' she said. 'There are so many of them. There's Fred . . . and Ruth . . . What's she doing here? Oh, I know!'

"An electric shock went through me. She had said 'Ruth'. Ruth was her cousin who had died suddenly the week before. But she had not been told of Ruth's sudden death.

"Chill after chill went up and down my spine. I felt on the verge of some powerful, almost frightening knowledge. She had murmured Ruth's name.

"Her voice was so surprisingly clear. 'It's so confusing! So many of them!' Suddenly her arms stretched out happily as when she had welcomed me. 'I'm going up,' she said."[10]

Another story was told by W. H. Ziegler[11] about his

grandmother, past eighty, who was not expected to live in the fall of 1959 although her mind was exceptionally active. Her youngest son Fred had been killed in a car accident shortly before, and this was followed by the death of her sister Louise. In both cases the family decided not to tell her about the deaths as she would only grieve, and they did not want to burden her last hours. The writer continued:

"My wife and I sat beside her during the final hours in the same room that Grandpa had died in nine years before.

"Suddenly Grandma sat straight up in bed, her eyes bright. She looked at me and said, 'Jim, get my dress quick; Pa is coming to take me with him. Hurry, Jim, hurry.'

"I took her frail old hand in mine and said, 'Yes, Grandma.'

"Then she leaned forward to peer out the window. 'He's here,' she said. 'Father is here.'

"I looked out the window but of course I saw no one. Nevertheless, I felt my scalp tighten and she said, 'Bless my soul! Fred and Louise are with him, and there's Mary Ann!' (Mary Ann was my mother.)

"A few minutes later as the doctor signed the death certificate I stood looking down at her. She wore a half smile and a look of utter content on her face."

This type of story, first collected and called 'Peak in Darien' cases by a Miss E. P. Cobbe almost a century ago, is the most convincing evidence that deathbed visions represent actual reality. As Alson Smith puts it:

"At least the eminent scientists, psychologists, and scholars who analyzed the phantoms and hallucinations for the Society for Psychical Research came to the conclusion that these so-called ghosts did indeed represent a genuine invasion by the deceased — an actual breaking through by conscious entities on the other side of the grave into the experience, the 'life space' of those still living. And no convincing alternative was ever offered."[12]

'Peak in Darien' refers to Keats' sonnet, 'On First Looking into Chapman's Homer', and compares the thrill of discovering this kind of evidence of the reality of a world just beyond us with that of the Spanish explorers who first saw the Pacific and

Looked at each other with a wild surmise —
Silent, upon a peak in Darien.

These stories are not as common as they used to be because the dying are usually taken to hospitals and given drugs to lessen any pain or the fear they are expected to have. Often their families are not present, but this has nothing to do with the validity of their experiences as pointers to what actually happens to the average person who dies peacefully. The fact that their families cannot know what is happening is no evidence either way.

It should be pointed out that a few dying persons see visions of the living, as Dr Osis reported in his monograph. Peak in Darien stories could thus be of the same nature were it not for the fact that in most of them the dying saw those they thought to be living along with those they knew to be dead as did Aubrey Eggleston in Chapter I, and that many of them expressed surprise or amazement at this.

If deathbed visions stood alone as the only manifestation of the life beyond, the Peak in Darien cases with the element of surprise usually involved would still be hard to explain on any other basis. As long as new examples continue to appear there is every reason to keep the issue open. However, there are other types of evidence that should be examined before we can state with any degree of assurance all that happens at death. So we keep on looking.

3 The Dead Are Raised

Yes, they are being raised today in ever-increasing numbers. This is not a discussion of reincarnation, but modern stories of those who, like Lazarus, are brought back from the dead, but unlike him, are able to remember and report what they experienced when dead, or supposedly dead. While the number of deathbed stories is decreasing because of modern medical practice, there are more reports of people who are so near death that their consciousness enters the next world before they are called back, remembering what had happened.

There are two reasons for the growing number of these experiences. One of them is the progress of medical knowledge by means of which many people who would formerly have been considered as beyond all hope of recovery are now restored to health. An example of this is the experience of Dr George Ritchie of Richmond, Virginia, which was written up in *Guideposts* in 1965 and told by him at the Spiritual Frontiers National Meeting in 1970.

As a lad he had just completed basic training in Camp Barkley, Texas, in December of 1943, when he was taken sick and died of lobar pneumonia (according to the medical report). For some reason the orderly persuaded the doctor on duty to inject a massive dose of adrenalin directly into the heart muscle. This was done nine minutes after he had been pronounced dead. The heart started again. What happened then was very dramatic and not inconsistent with the reports of deathbed scenes in the previous chapter.

The point made here is that modern medicine has made possible a great number of similar recoveries through chest surgery, adrenalin, heart massage, electrical stimuli and heart transplants. Sometimes the patient recovers and is able to give his version of what seemed to happen to him during this period of unconsciousness.

The cousin of a house guest of mine had an experience similar to that of Dr Ritchie. "Ethel had a heart attack during the war at Newport Beach, California. The doctor came and said that the heart had stopped, but he continued to work and she finally recovered. Afterward she reported how wonderful it was, that everything was beautiful, and she was ready to go at any time; indeed, she would welcome death when it came."

The other reason for the great increase in the number who apparently go into the life beyond and return when it seems medically impossible is the growth of the spiritual healing movement. While the early church believed in and practised healing through prayer and the laying on of hands, scientific medicine had practically usurped the field until the rise of Christian Science. Now the Pentecostal movements have moved into the same area, though with a very different philosophy and technique, and some of the same faith and practice have spilled over into the more traditional churches, especially the Episcopal. Recent developments in both depth psychology and physics (as outlined in Chapter II) have cleared away some of the so-called scientific obstacles and have made the practice intellectually respectable and therefore practicable.

The recovery of Aubrey Eggleston from almost certain death (see Chapter I) apparently came as a result of the prayers of his wife and her prayer partner. Mrs Eggleston claims that the Lord had to put the doctor to sleep to get him out of the way while the healing took place. In the case of Mrs Grohe (also told in Chapter I), a more recent medical discovery, an electric shock, was used to restart the heart.

In this same general category there are four cases, including Lazarus, in the New Testament, and three about Elijah and Elisha in the Old Testament, but no details are given about what happened in the minds of the persons involved. The majority were children or young people, and some may have been only unconscious, like the daughter of the ruler of the synagogue (Luke 8:52) and Eutychus (Acts 20:10). There are many others from the ancient world, shading into legend and mythology, but the only one that carries the sense of reality of the modern stories is the following one:

Plutarch, writing about AD 79 when the New Testament was being formed, told the story of Aridaeus, a soldier of Asia Minor, who had a severe fall and became unconscious. When he eventually recovered he claimed that he had been fully conscious all the time and had seen and spoken with dead kinsmen who told him he was not really dead because apparently he was still "made fast to the body". Eventually Aridaeus' soul body re-entered his physical body. He described the process as "like suddenly being sucked through a tube".[1]

Dr Robert Crookall has collected[2] about fifty-five stories of what he calls the 'pseudo-dead', that is, people who were unconscious through sickness, anaesthetics, or accident, as far as observers could see, and who were sometimes pronounced medically dead. After they recovered, however, they practically all agreed that they were fully conscious the whole time, but had left their bodies and were in another place or plane of existence. I will summarize a few similar stories from various sources in order that we may get the 'feel' of them. Later on we will discuss their meaning and validity.

The earliest to be carefully investigated by the Society for Psychical Research is that of Dr A. S. Wiltse of Skiddy, Kansas, which was first reported in the *St. Louis Medical and Surgical Journal,* November 1889. I condense it from F. W. H. Myers' *Human Personality.*[3] The doctor was thought to be dying of typhoid fever in the summer of 1889, but recovered and later wrote as follows:

"I bid adieu to my family and friends and soon sank into utter unconsciousness . . . I passed about four hours in all without pulse or perceptible heart-beat, as I was later informed by Dr S. H. Raynes who was the only physician present. He thrust a needle deep into my flesh at different points but got no response . . .

"I came again into a state of conscious existence . . . I

realized my condition and reasoned thus: I have died, and yet I am as much a man as ever . . . I seemed to be perfectly naked, but on reaching the door found myself clothed. As I turned, to my surprise the arm of one of the gentlemen present passed through mine without apparent resistance. I looked at my body (still lying on the bed) and was surprised at the paleness of the face.

"I turned and passed out the open door, and into the street. Then I discovered that I had become larger than in earth life, and congratulated myself. I am somewhat smaller in body than I just like to be, but in the next life, I thought, I am to be as I desire. My clothes, I noticed, had accommodated themselves to my increased stature, and I fell to wondering where they came from.

" 'How well I feel!' I thought. 'Only a few minutes ago I was horribly sick and distressed. Then came the change called death which I have so much dreaded. It is past now and here I am still a man, alive and thinking, yes, thinking as clearly as ever. I shall never be sick again. I have no more to die.' And in sheer exuberance of spirits I danced a figure . . . I discovered then a small cord, like a spider's web, running from my shoulders back to my body and attaching to it at the base of the neck in front.

"I had walked only a few steps down the street when again I lost consciousness . . . and found myself alighting gently on the beginning of a narrow, well-built roadway. After this I seemed to feel rather than to hear a voice, 'This is the road to the eternal world. Yonder rocks are the boundary line between the two worlds. Once you pass them you can no more return into the body . . .'

"My eyes opened. I looked at my hands and then at the little white cot on which I was lying, and in astonishment and disappointment exclaimed, 'What in the world has happened to me? Must I die again?' "

Myers and the Society for Psychical Research knew of only one other similar experience which had occured before the publication of *Human Personality* in 1901. Here is a sample of the many collected by Crookall.[4] A fireman, S. Bourne, whose fire station suffered a direct hit from a bomb during the war, gave his experience:

"I heard a roar and was out of my body. I could see my earth body lying under a joist. I was five feet above it, 'free as air'. I had a form. I felt no pain. I was conscious of every detail in the room. One of my colleagues had been sitting by the window. 'I must get back and help her,' I thought, and with what I can only describe as a thunderclap, I was back in the body. . . . I must have been functioning in my spiritual body. I shall never forget that glorious feeling of freedom and lightness. If this is death, why worry?"

The first story of this kind which came to my attention as one to be taken seriously is found in the autobiography of Louis Tucker,[5] an Episcopal clergyman from the South. Inasmuch as I have never seen any reference to it I will quote, at random and in some detail, from the passage.

"In the spring of 1909 I was desperately ill at Baton Rouge of ptomaine poisoning . . .

"I knew the end was in sight. Curiously enough I, who had been afraid of so many things, was not afraid of this. . . . The sensation was not quite like anything earthly . . . There was the same sense of hurrying blackness, of rapid transition . . . swift readjustment. Death is a very much overrated process.

"I emerged into a place where many people were being met by friends. It was quiet and full of light, and Father was waiting for me. He looked exactly as he had in the least years of his life and wore the last suit of clothes he had owned . . .

"Soon I discovered that we were not talking, but thinking. . . He thought a question, I an answer without speaking; the process was practically instantaneous . . . I wanted to know how he was, if he had a home in the city, if he had yet settled to any definite work there . . . I gathered that not only his clothes but his appearance were different when he worked, that he did have a home, which we should share, that he had glorious friends, that he had some definite employment, and many more things . . .

"At last there came a pause, and I wished to go through the gate into the city.

"Just then someone behind us called out . . . What he said was in ideas, not words: if I were to go back at all I must go at once. Until then, the idea that I might go back had not occurred to either of us. I did not want to go back . . . The parish could get another man as good as I . . . Susie could live without me until she came over, too; she would miss me dreadfully . . . But my little children, without a father to take care of them! What would the children do? At that moment, though I did not know it, Susie was kneeling in the church and asking the same question of God . . . I turned to Father for guidance; as usual. He gave none. It was my problem between me and God . . .

"He then referred the whole matter to Our Father. I did not know how . . . the answer came to both of us. It was 'Go back!' . . .

"Instantly we were at peace . . . I swung into the darkness again, as a man might swing on a train, thoroughly disgusted that I could not stay, and absolutely certain that it was right for me to go back . . .

"I came to, to find myself lying on my bed with the doctor bending over telling me that I was safe now and would live . . . The doctor had arrived and pronounced me dead, and so had two others. Susie would not have it so and insisted that he try an injection of heart stimulant — adrenalin, I think. He did so and the heart started up again . . ."

Note that this happened when Dr Tucker was thirty-six, and was published in a much longer form when he was about seventy.

The *Edinburgh Medical Journal* for June 1937 (pages 75-83) has a paper which was presented by Sir Auckland Geddes to the Royal Medical Society about a man who apparently died and was later forced back into his body by medical treatment, remembering everything: "Although I had no body I had what appeared to be perfect two-eyed vision. I understood from my mentor that our brains are just end organs projecting, as it were, from the three dimensional universe into the psychic stream. Gradually I realized that I could see not only my body and the bed on which it was, but everything in the whole house and garden, and in London, and Scotland."

Gene Albright of Yarnell, Arizona, told of his death and resurrection in *Fate* magazine. After describing his death at 12:03 am on 9 December 1960, he continued:

"Suddenly the darkness cleared. My mind seemed sharper and clearer than it had ever been. Just as suddenly the pain was no more. With this I felt wonderfully and supremely free. And I was no longer alone.

"It was then I heard my wife softly, from the very bottom of her heart, praying for me. I looked closer and realized something very startling. I was hearing the words of her silent prayer. Besides this there were dozens of people in the room with her. I have never known such beautiful, radiant people.

"I called to my wife. She didn't hear me, so I spoke louder. Still she did not hear or respond. I asked the closest person to explain what had happened, and where had all these people come from. It isn't possible to put into words the pure love and oneness I experienced as I turned my attention to this person. He spoke no words to me. I just knew, directly and exactly, the answers to my questions. *I knew I was dead.* Memories, long forgotten, returned. The people in the room were people I had known when I was young, but since had forgotten.

"Time had ceased to be important. I could 'see' in either direction with ease. Yesterday and tomorrow were two parts of the same time. I could see energies, forms, and inter-locking fields of the most beautiful colors and sounds, greater than the finest music ever played by masters.

"During the death experience I learned that in exactly seven minutes of normal, conscious time I would return to my body and consciousness. In this very short time I learned more than in my entire previous 34 years. I learned what love is and how it works. I realized that life energy is itself love. I focused on the beautiful love of my wife, and her warmth, and then went back through into consciousness. As I did everything else faded away. The pain returned and the long battle began again. I opened my eyes.

"And I had lost something, something I had lived with most of my life — fear.

"The doctor, finally located the next morning, told my wife that mine was a hopeless case. 'I have never tried to treat a dead man before. I can't understand how he is alive at all.' "

The author goes on to tell how he was guided back to health the following months, and of the transformation of his consciousness, and of the meaning and purpose of his life.

Another example of a similar story is reported by Harold Sherman.[6] In this case, instead of witnesses, Gratz Baily, aged forty-five, left a letter addressed to his mother and written several hours before his passing. Sherman has a photostat of it.

"Dear Mother:

"I returned from the afterlife last night — and came home only to stay a few days. Am in hopes of leaving some time in the morning.

"I am satisfied. Would like to see you all before I go — but can't. Death should have no terror. Everyone that comes here — knows. Made two trips last night.

"I'm glad you can't stay long at best. Only a little pain and all is over. Laugh at Death when he comes. Death we dread just because we don't know it.

"I would never shed a tear over any of you again. Will see you soon. Come on — I have found the way.

"Gratz"

He sent this letter from Hugo, Oklahoma, where he died, to his mother in Sebree, Kansas. He was a graduate of the University of Kentucky, and had never been known to have had psychic experiences.

Dr Shafika Karagulla, a psychiatrist researching what she calls Higher Sense Perception, tells this story about a dinner party in Washington to discuss HSP where there were two physicians, a member of Congress, an ambassador and a number of government people:

"The member of Congress who was present made a great impression on the group. She related in simple and dramatic words a personal experience with HSP. Years before her son had been at the point of death. There were several persons in the room praying for his recovery. At a certain point all those present saw a bright light which startled them, and at the same time the young man obviously took a sudden turn for the worse. All present earnestly and insistently renewed their prayers for his recovery. Although the young man had appeared, without any doubt, to be dying, he suddenly began to show signs of recovery. In a few days he was well along the road to health. His recovery seemed so amazing that his mother cautiously asked whether anything had happened at the moment when he appeared to come back from the very door of death.

"Her son said he remembered clearly what had happened and he would tell her if she would make him a promise. She must never again try to recall him if he were at the point of passing out of this life. She made the promise. Then he told her rather sadly that as he was leaving his body, he passed into a realm of great splendor and ease of movement and clear mental perception. The prayers of his mother and his friends had pulled him back and it was like coming into a dark prison cell to come back to consciousness in the physical body. The son is today a member of Congress."[7]

The research project by Dr Karlis Osis mentioned earlier also included some questions about very sick patients in order, as far as possible, to compare their experiences with those of terminal patients. Without going into detail I will quote the conclusions of the study in this respect:

"When revived persons did see visions, these were quite in line with other cases in our survey. If anything there appeared to be only increased intensity of beauty and happiness, that is, a difference of degree, not of quality . . . Characteristic responses were, 'Why did you bring me back, Doc? It was so nice there.' 'I want to go back. Let me go back.' The visual contents varied widely but the associated emotional qualities of whar might be called transcendental were quite constant: inexpressible beauty, peace, and happiness. These revived patients intensely desire death, that is, to return to the experience of indescribable beauty and peace connected with dying."[8]

My comment here has to do with the "increased intensity of beauty and peace" reported as compared with the experiences of terminal patients. It seems that those who are revived and can remember their vision are able to give a fuller and more detailed account than the dying who had no opportunity in most cases to give any particulars. Although there is no inconsistency between them, there are two other differences. Those who come back almost always demonstrate a change in consciousness and character which of course can not be seen in the dying. Most important is the conquest of all fear, so they look forward with joyous expectancy toward the life beyond. The other difference is that they are not merely able to be more detailed in their reports, but in some cases they feel definitely they have been given a mission to prepare others who have not had their opportunity for the next great step in life — which is death. This was certainly true of Gene Albright, Aubrey Eggleston and Dr Ritchie.

I cannot resist a brief quotation from an article by David Snell.[9] Writing on 'How It Feels to Die' after being brought back from apparent death from penicillin shock, he says: "There is something else, something that I felt, or experienced, or beheld at the very last instant. What was it? I knew it so well when it was there opening to me, something more beautiful, more gentle, more loving than the mind or imagination of a living creature could ever conceive."

Did David Snell glimpse what Francis Thompson was reaching after in 'The Hound of Heaven'?

> I dimly guess what Time in mists confounds:
> Yet ever and anon a trumpet sounds
> From the hid battlements of Eternity;
> Those shaken mists a space unsettle, then
> Round the half-glimpsed turrets slowly wash again.

4 There are also Ghosts

There are ghosts? Yes, and phantoms, apparitions, visions, dreams, voices! How far into superstition do we have to go? Surely we can't think of such things as the dead speaking to us, or can we? I do not know. Once I was sure that there was nothing real in these 'superstitions', as I called them, for an intelligent person in this scientific age. This scientific age? I finally decided that this was just the reason I had to examine stories of the dead reporting back — ghost stories, if you please. I could not be scientific without at least considering them. Such thinking requires that we begin with the facts. No evidence is to be by-passed no matter how wild and unscientific it first seems to be.

I must confess that I was tempted not to discuss this, but instead I am burying it right in the middle of the book. It may be too far out to get a fair reading from most of the people I hope to reach. However, I am not writing science fiction, but science — science about matters which most of us have been taught to be beyond the reach of any science. We cannot be sure until we honestly examine the evidence. If ghosts have anything to tell us about the waiting world it is essential that we listen to them. Let's begin with a series of stories: experiences and incidents from persons whose integrity is beyond question, and who also have a reputation for sound judgement.

First I shall relate a series of experiences of Dr Harold Paul Sloan, for many years a prominent Methodist pastor in Philadelphia.

"It was fifteen years ago. I was calling on a young woman, Dorothy Williams. As I entered her chamber she was in a state of marked exaltation, of which the outward explanation was a vivid manifestation of her father from heaven. He had come to her holding one of her little dead brothers by the hand and carrying the other one. Mr Williams had said to her, 'Dot, watch your step. You are going to be all right.'

"Dorothy had been married about a year, and her own little first baby had died two weeks before. When death took her baby and seemed to be approaching for her, her first reaction was one of bitter resentment and great fear. She felt that God had been unfair. Then this vision had come and everything was changed. She was so poised and elevated that I marvelled.

"As she related the story of the visit of her father I wondered if her experience could be real. To test her I asked her if she had seen anything of her own little baby. I thought that if this vision was a product of her imagination, her grieving mother's heart would certainly have produced an appearance of her child. In response to my question Dorothy answered, 'No, I did not see anything of my baby. I looked all over for him, and he was nowhere to be seen. But father said that when I reached heaven I would find him.'

"Then as we talked she had another vision of being out under the open sky, surrounded by stars and baby hands. I asked her, 'Dorothy, what is heaven like?' She replied, 'I am not in heaven, just out under the stars.'

"Then the vision faded and Dorothy said to her mother and pastor, 'If Jesus wants me to live, I want to live; but He will have to hurry for I am so tired I can't live much longer.' Two hours later she died."[1]

This story could just as well have been classified amongst the deathbed visions, as that is what it is, except that what happened took place several hours before death, so that it becomes a ghost story. Indeed there is little difference between some deathbed visions and ghost stories, but we find it easier to accept visions told by the dying than those told under more ordinary circumstances. In the presence of the mystery of death other mysteries seem more natural and to be expected.

Dr Louisa Rhine has gathered and organized a great mass of spontaneous material. Here is a typical incident.

"A young American in the Air Force during World War II had entered the service several years after his mother's death, and was a tail gunner on a B29. He had been flying in missions over Europe, and one night they were returning to their base after completing a bombing mission. All the crew except the pilots were asleep when in a dream the gunner saw his mother standing on the tip of one wing of his plane. She was dressed in white flowing robes and calling his name, warning him of danger. She begged him to awake, the danger was very near. Her voice was far away and echoed in his dream; yet it was so realistic that he awoke to find a German fighter plane flying directly above their B29 and out of vision of the pilot and co-pilot. With the rest of the crew asleep, no one would have known the enemy was there. He felt that had it not been for his mother's warning, neither he nor the crew members would have escaped."[2]

F. W. H. Myers also has many similar stories, most of them carefully investigated and confirmed by the Society for Psychical Research. Here is an extract of one of his best.

"A traveling salesman, writing out his morning orders in a hotel room in St Joseph, Missouri, at noon with bright sunshine in the room, saw his sister, who had died nine years previously, sitting at the table beside him. He later wrote, 'I was startled and dumfounded, almost doubting my senses, but the cigar in my mouth and pen in my hand, with the ink still wet on my letter, satisfied me that I had not been dreaming but was wide awake. She appeared as if alive. Her eyes looked kindly and perfectly naturally into mine. Her skin was so life-like I could see the glow of moisture on its surface.'

"This visitation so impressed him that he took the next train home, and related to his family what had happened. His father was inclined to ridicule the story, but his mother almost fainted when he told of a bright red scratch on her right cheek. It seemed that in preparing the body her mother had accidentally scratched her, but had been able to cover it with powder so nobody else knew anything about it.

"Several weeks later the mother died happy in her belief that she would rejoin her favorite child in a better world. At the same time the salesman felt that his sister had come to him partly so that he would return home and see his mother before her unexpected death."[3]

Leslie Weatherhead, an English minister, vouches for the following story:

"A minister was sitting alone in his study one night when he heard the bell ring. Going to the door he found standing there a young woman whom he knew fairly well. She was from a village some five miles away, which was on a circuit from which the minister had moved sixteen months before.

" 'Good evening,' she cried, 'I expect you have forgotten me, but I have come on a very urgent errand. My father is dying. He never attended church much, but once or twice we persuaded him to hear you preach. I do wish you would come and pray with him before he passes away.'

" 'I will come at once,' the minister replied. Putting on his hat and coat and taking an umbrella, he set out on a five mile walk, accompanied by the young woman.

"On his arrival at the house the wife greeted him warmly. 'How good of you to come, but how did you know that my husband was passing away?'

" 'Your daughter came for me,' he replied with some surprise at the question. It was the woman's turn to be surprised now.

" 'Come upstairs at once,' she said, 'and we will talk afterwards.'

"The minister went to the bedside of the dying man, spoke to him and prayed with him, and shortly afterwards the end came. Turning to the woman he asked where the daughter was, for he had not seen her since they entered the house. The woman replied, 'I was surprised when you said that my daughter called, and that you had come together. You had not heard then that my daughter died a year ago?'

"Now the minister was astonished indeed. 'Dead!' he exclaimed, 'She came to my door, rang the bell, and walked out here with me. But there,' he said, 'I think that I can prove that. As we came along together the road was torn up in one place, and a watchman and another man were sitting in front of a fire. They saw us go by. I'll speak to them on my way home.'

"He set off on his return journey, and found the two men still sitting in front of a fire. 'You saw me go by an hour or so ago, didn't you?' he said to the men. 'Was I alone?'

" 'Yes, sir,' one of them replied, 'and you were talking away to yourself as fast as you could go.' "[4]

Charles Hampton relates the only traditional ghost story which I shall quote:

"Mrs C. D. Diehl of Omaha tells the following story from her home town in Sweden. A certain Mrs Greta Pearson living there became ill and died. Shortly afterwards Mrs Pearson was seen as an apparition at various times by numbers of the villagers. She was usually seen in the open between the house and the barn. Mr Jacob Erickson, an uncle of Mrs Pearson, never having seen the ghost, was anxious to accost the late Mrs Pearson, and he determined, if successful, to have a chat with the ghost and find out what she wanted. He was successful, and the following conversation took place between the living and the dead:

"Mr Erickson said, 'What's the matter with you? Don't you know you are disturbing the whole neighborhood?'

"The ghost replied, 'Oh, I'm so thankful you spoke to me. I'm Mrs Greta Pearson who just died.'

" 'Yes, I know,' he said, 'and you are causing a lot of talk.'

"She replied, 'When I was living I used to steal money from my husband. I kept it hidden in a handkerchief in the barn, and no one knows where to look for it. I can't rest till that money is restored to my husband. If I point out the place will you promise to recover it and return it to him?'

"Mr Erickson gave his word and the ghost pointed out the place. As it was dark and the task required a ladder, Mr Erickson waited until morning. He then related the incident to the mayor, the postmaster, and the doctor in the village, and with these witnesses he recovered the money and restored it to the husband who was completely ignorant of the wife's pilferings, and had not missed the money since it had been taken a little at a time.

"The ghost of Mrs Pearson, troubled no longer — earth-bound no longer — was not seen again."[5]

Harold Sherman tells the story of his male nurse friend, David Quinn.[6] David's friendship with Sherman grew out of a common interest in psychic matters discovered while the latter was recovering from surgery in Battle Creek, Michigan. They corresponded for a while but lost touch during World War I. Then in January 1919 Sherman had a nightmarish dream or vision in which he saw his friend David leaning over him with great yearning, apparently trying to speak, but no words could be heard. The experience was repeated the next two nights with even greater intensity, so that Harold cried out as David was trying desperately to say something to him. But his form dissolved in the darkness leaving Harold with the sad conviction that he would never see his old friend again in this life.

Harold tried to reach David at the last address he had, but the letter was returned. However, three weeks later he received two letters from mutual friends telling of David's death on the morning of 21 January after having been in a deep coma for three days — the same three during which Sherman had had his visions. One of them was from a nurse whose letter contained this statement: "It is strange, but on each of the three nights prior to David's passing, he appeared at my bedside. I knew he was in trouble and calling to me, and I would have gone to him at once if I had only known where he was."

Our final story in this series is taken from Dr Frederick E. Chamberlain, a chiropractor who came to Los Angeles from New Zealand in 1896.

"On the morning in question I was sitting quietly at my desk. Feeling someone had entered the room, I turned, and there, to my amazement and astonishment, stood my mother, as real and complete as I had ever beheld her in human life. She had passed to the other side of life many years before, yet she spoke to me:

" 'Fred, Sam is in trouble; send him some money.'

" 'How much?' I inquired.

" 'Sixty dollars,' she responded.

" 'I shall do so at once,' I answered. She then departed.

"Sam was my younger brother and I had not heard from him for many years. He lived in Christchurch, New Zealand, and at that time there were mail boats only twice a month, which took a month to reach South Island. My mother knew nothing before she died of American money or exchange. However, I immediately wrote to my brother Sam, explaining the circumstances and enclosing a twelve pound money order, the equivalent of sixty dollars in those days. Three months later I received in response a letter from him saying:

" 'Fred, this is beyond me. I am amazed, startled, bewildered, for I had about concluded that this life ended all, and that death was final, the end for us, but this revelation is so convincing, overpowering, and profound that it has knocked all my theories of life and death sideways. . .

" 'I was sick with rheumatic fever, and could not get out of bed. We were buying our home on an acre of land. Fred, the money arrived here just one day ahead of an impending catastrophe, for early the next morning a rap on the door was heard and my wife answered. There stood the Sheriff with the real estate owner from whom I was buying the place.

" ' "Mr Chamberlain, I have a very unpleasant duty to perform as I hold here an order from the Court to put you and your furniture on the sidewalk for the twelve pound installment you owe this realtor."

" 'My wife handed him the twelve pounds you had just sent me, and took a receipt. . . .' "[7]

So here are seven stories (nine if we include the vision of the smiling Philip and the experience of Anna mentioned in Chapter I), all of which claim to be manifestations of the dead or dying for a variety of good reasons. They are samples of hundreds which might be told, the majority of them coming close to the time of death, according to the studies made by Dr Robert Crookall. Most of these occurring at the time of death simply give the fact that it has taken place and bring comfort and assurance to a close relative or friend, like the wife of a man I met last week. They were living in Tientsin, China, when she suddenly felt the presence of her stepfather, and said to her husband with great emotion,

"Daddy Joe is dead!" Weeks later when the mail came from the States her sure knowledge was confirmed. He had died just at the time she knew it.

But I have chosen more varied types to illustrate various other motives, to confirm and extend our knowledge of the life beyond, and to strengthen faith by using cases where there are corroborating witnesses. In this discussion we will skip the cases of Philip, Anna and Dorothy which are of the most common comforting type and for which there is no proof except as one knows the individuals involved and the differences the experiences made in their lives. The other six are quite different.

Each of these contain elements of fact and of purpose unknown to the person or persons who had the experience. The timing and the form were apparently necessary to attain the desired result. Each of them was sufficiently impressive and evidential to accomplish their purpose. The mother of the gunner appeared in a dream, if that is what it was, and was able to save her son and the rest of the crew. The sister of the salesman not only prepared her mother for death, but brought faith to all of the family by her scratched cheek, known only to the mother. The daughter of the dying man was most remarkable in ringing a bell and accompanying the minister on a five-mile walk. Not only were the circumstances as she said, but the statement of the watchman strongly confirms it. The Swedish ghost has the most questionable heritage of any of these stories. It is too bad that the Society for Psychical Research did not query witnesses and get signed statements of the people involved. However, if it involved any matter of common acceptance, nobody would seriously doubt it. The finding of the money really clinched the matter.

Harold Sherman's story of the thrice repeated and very emotional appearances of David is especially interesting because they apparently took place before death. Neither Harold nor his nurse friend, Miss Macheracker, knew that David was alone and dying in a strange city hundreds of miles away, yet they had the same vision on the same three nights. The motive is clear. (The significance of the timing will be discussed in a later chapter.)

The final story of the Chamberlains and their mother carries even more interesting suggestions. Not only had she kept in touch with her sons on opposite sides of the earth, but she knew the problem that Sam would be facing many weeks in advance. Apparently she had also kept up with many other factors, the exchange of money between dollars and pounds and the steamer and mail schedules, for example. And like the Swedish ghost and the daughter of the dying man, she had to not only appear visually but to carry on a conversation.

While none of these stories go beyond the implications of the deathbed scenes and the reports of the 'pseudo-dead', as Crookall calls them, they do add certainty and strength from some angles. They demonstrate that the deceased are still very much alive, still care for friends and relatives, know what is happening to them and want to be of help. Three of them indicate that they have a sense of future events. We may see into or sometimes visit the next world, but these stories show that those who have gone on may at times come back and manifest themselves effectively in this world. Historically the most famous examples of this are the resurrection appearances of Jesus. As in most of our stories, so here also he appeared only to those who loved him. One incident also indicates that we cannot escape conscience by death, and sometimes may suffer until we have righted old wrongs. (This will be discussed farther in the chapter on hell.)

It is hard to see how these reports can be entirely imaginary. Nor can they be fictional in most of the cases when the character and the standing of their sources is taken into consideration. All but that of Harold Sherman require the motive and the knowledge which only a deceased person could supply. There is simply no other rational explanation. Even in Sherman's case it cannot be called clairvoyance because it was also shared by another person far away and at the same time. Any one of these reports, standing by itself, could easily be questioned, but with not only the other five of the more dramatic ones, and hundreds of others which I myself have come to know of out of the thousands which are known, the case for the dead returning at times as visions, voices, apparitions and in dreams, to comfort, guide, instruct, protect, or get help from the living is almost watertight for any honest and intelligent person.

Other stories (not included) indicate that sometimes contact is made through children or strangers when close friends cannot be impressed. For example, J. B. Rhine tells a tale of a four-year-old playing with a pencil and paper, who was actually writing a shorthand letter of great importance from the father who had died very suddenly without giving his wife some information essential for the settling of his estate and her welfare. The only truth we can be sure of in all these reports is that no two of them will be alike. Yet all of them carry elements of a common truth — that we can be sure of the reality and goodness of the waiting world.

I have not discussed haunted houses nor the more typical ghost stories associated with them. The reason is not the lack of such stories, nor that they are probably not true in many cases. Rather, the field is so large and complicated, and would lead only to controversy and probably rejection of our primary thesis by many intelligent people. Nor is it necessary that we talk about poltergeists, demon possession, vampires, spooks, etc. Some of these will be mentioned briefly in the chapter dealing with hell, but for the readers of this book none of these have any relation to the waiting world as they will find it. Of course if one is contemplating murder or suicide and is closed to all ideas of a good and loving God it might be well to heed the warning of Jesus (Luke 12:43): "When the unclean spirit has gone out of a man, he passes through waterless places seeking rest, but he finds none." Certainly no person has reached this far in this book who can remain so ignorant or evil as to suffer such a fate.

Returning to our main theme, what shall we conclude from these tall tales of the dead speaking in so many and varied fashions? Perhaps only this: they give us other glimpses of the next life consistent with those we have already had from deathbeds and returning travellers. The picture may be much clearer and more detailed when the evidence from reports from so-called astral travellers and mediums has been set out too. But in the meantime let it be said that faith is like a grain of mustard which, if watered, will become a tree providing shade and shelter. And even a ghost can water a mustard seed!

5 Travellers from Earth

We have now looked briefly through three of the five windows purporting to give glimpses of the life beyond. In Chapter II we sensed not only some of the eagerness of the dying as their eyes seemed to penetrate, even dimly, the utter splendour that lay beyond, but also their joyous response to the welcome of their beloved dead. Next we heard the more specific reports of those who apparently died, but were brought or sent back to finish their work in the physical body. Then in Chapter IV we discovered that the dead return in one way or other to comfort or aid the living, or to complete a task, or correct a mistake in the earth life just ended.

Two windows, perhaps the most important of all, remain to be examined before we attempt to outline some more specific conclusions about the world that is waiting for each one of us. The first, which we shall consider here is the report of those who are reputed to be able to leave their bodies, as the Apostle Paul did when he visited Paradise and the third heaven, and give us descriptions of the lands ahead.

The phrase 'travellers from earth' is an attempt to describe an experience for which there is no adequate expression in English — or any other language as far as I know. The more usual terms 'astral travel' and 'astral projection' are neither one accurate, saying either too much or too little. It is based on a theory, already mentioned but not yet discussed, that one has more than one body, and that under some circumstances one (the real person, the center of consciousness, or the soul) may leave the physical body and function in a soul or spirit body, sometimes bringing back memories on return.

For example, it is often claimed that the feeling of familiarity we have about places visited for the first time is the result of having been there in our dreams. I do not know.

More common and evidential are stories similar to the brief one mentioned at the beginning of Chapter I of the woman who saw her unconscious body from over the head of the hospital bed. Hundreds of these have been reported, often with strongly supporting evidence. But these are not travellers *from* earth, but *on* earth, although they are equally out-of-the-body experiences. Several of these will be told because their evidence can be checked and confirmed, thus suggesting that those beyond the physical are also in touch with reality, especially when they confirm and amplify what has already been learned from other sources.

There are apparently three types of situation in which the spiritual body or bodies may leave: *forced, willed* and *called* from outside of ourselves. The *forced* type includes apparent death (as in Chapter V), accidents and shock where we are knocked unconscious and accept death, extreme weakness, anaesthesia, and possibly hypnosis which also requires our willingness and co-operation in most cases. *Willed* astral projection includes that which comes through various exercises and disciplines such as that of Hindu Yogis, and some modern experimenters, but also some 'sensitives' who are able at will to journey into another realm of consciousness.

It is sometimes difficult to distinguish between some of the more gifted of these people and those who are *called* from the other world. Some dreams are surely in the latter category, and possibly much of mystical experience and inspiration. Clairvoyance may be similar to inspiration. There are no studies familiar to me[1] which adequately and persuasively cover this field as a whole.

My first information about astral projection was from the autobiography of Ed Morrell. He was a young member of a 'Robin-Hoodish' gang of bandits who delighted in holding up Southern Pacific trains in the San Joaquin Valley of California while aiding some of the political victims during the period when the state was controlled by the Southern Pacific machine. The outlaws were finally captured and Morrell was sentenced to life imprisonment, and then com-

mitted to solitary confinement when falsely convicted of
smuggling guns into San Quentin prison. While undergoing
straitjacket torture to force him to reveal the location of
non-existent guns, he had a mystical experience and learned
to leave his body when trussed in two straitjackets without
food or water for days on end. Twenty-four members of the
band had died under this treatment, but he was the twenty-
fifth whom they tried to kill — hence the title of his autobiography, *The Twenty-Fifth Man*. But let him tell some of
his own story.[2]

"In those early experiments with the power of projection I
was dreadfully obsessed with the belief that I was Ed Morrell,
my real physical self, and not a spectre, a mere phantom, a
shadow that had left the jacket and the dungeon. I reasoned,
'I can walk, I can see, I can hear, I can smell, I can feel! More,
I can talk.' But I could not explain to my mind why people
never answered me when I addressed them. Their indifference
nonplussed me, because I believed they heard.
"There were many discrepancies, incongruous, incompatible with logic and reason. For instance, I could look through
people as if I were an X-ray. Opacity meant nothing to me. I
could flit through doors without opening them. Solid walls
were as tissue paper, intangible, non-existent, when I wished
to pass beyond. A moving train going at the highest speed
was just an ordinary escalator to me to step on and off at
will. And yet all this never appeared to be other than real."

Only after he was released from solitary confinement was
Morrell able to confirm that many of his experiences had
taken place as he had seen them, including the wrecking of a
steamer outside the Golden Gate. Years later he married a girl
with whom he had fallen in love on one of those excursions
while his body was supposed to be dying in a prison dungeon.
This account, which became the basis for Jack London's *Star
Rover*, was too much for me to take seriously at the time I
read it, but I put it on a shelf in my memory, forgotten until
recently when I realized that it was not science fiction but an
actuality which I could now accept, and which would make a
good introduction to this chapter.

Now take one experience of Carl Jung, the noted psycho-analyst:

"Jung had broken his foot and then had a heart attack. For some time he lingered between life and death, and it was then that he had a series of momentous nightly visions. 'Once,' he wrote, 'it seemed to me that I was high up in space. Far below I saw the globe of earth, bathed in a glorious blue light. In many places the globe seemed colored, or spotted dark green like oxydized silver. Far away to the left lay a broad expanse — the reddish-yellow desert of Arabia. Then it was as though the silver of the earth had assumed a reddish-gold hue. Beyond was the Red Sea, and far, far back — as if in the upper left of a map — I could just make out a bit of the Mediterranean . . .'

"Jung estimated that in order to have had so broad a view of the world, he would have had to be a thousand miles up. 'The sight of the earth from this height was the most glorious thing I have ever seen,' he said.

"Of the whole series of episodes Jung wrote: 'It is impossible to convey the beauty and intensity of emotion during those visions. They were the most tremendous things I have ever experienced.' Although he called them visions, he said of them, 'I would never have imagined that any such experience was possible. It was not a product of imagination. The visions and experiences were utterly real; there was nothing subjective about them; they had a quality of absolute objectivity.' "[3]

As I read these stories and scores of others like them recounted by Raynor Johnson, DeWitt Smith, Robert Crookall and others, it seemed to me that they had nothing to do with the waiting world, or what happens at death. They were another class of way-out phenomena that I would not have to discuss, and most certainly not defend, in the same class as flying saucers and astrology. Then about this time I read Emmanuel Swedenborg's *Heaven and Hell* and asked myself the meaning of the Apostle Paul's experience of being taken up into the third heaven to be discussed from another angle in Chapter XI. I began again to examine some of the works of the mystics, and to look at some of my own experiences in a different light.

It soon became clear to me that here was another approach or window to the life beyond which I dared not ignore. While the examples so far given deal with our familiar world, the persons involved are clearly in another dimension or level of existence. Material obstacles are no obstacle; nor do they ordinarily have power by either voice or touch to make themselves known to those in the physical dimension. But they seem at times to contact a spiritual world, and persons who have died are solid to them. Sometimes they can speak to each other.

Dr Shafika Karagulla tells about a mid-Western physician who claimed that he had been given amazing diagnostic powers through a series of dream experiences which take us a very long step beyond those of Jung. He finally agreed to relate them for the record, but only on condition that nothing should be said about them until he had passed on. As Dr Karagulla tells it:

"Dr Philip could see any organ in the patient's body and observe its function and any pathology that might be present. He knew the complete condition of his patient in the first few minutes as the person sat before him in his office. In order to protect his medical standing he said nothing about this and always put the patient through routine laboratory tests before giving the diagnosis . . .

"Dr Philip spent two days giving the history of his early experiences and the gradual improvement of his abilities through the years. He said that for many years he had regularly attended 'classes' when he was asleep at night. During the sleep state he found himself in what appeared to be a medical college where night after night clear and logical medical lectures were given in perfectly intelligent sequence with none of the confusion or irrelevancies that normally accompany a dream state. He spoke with individuals and professors who were present in these classes and discussed medical problems. He felt as alert and as aware as he did in waking consciousness and on waking could remember everything that had been said. In these classes he was trained to see into the physical bodies of his patients when he was wide awake in his office as easily as he did in the night classes when he was asleep."[4]

Dr Karagulla also describes how Dr Philip, who was frequently called in as a consultant at the Mayo Clinic, was able to demonstrate his ability with people he had never seen, and that he was always proved correct by medical records and later tests by more conventional diagnostic procedures.

In this case I would throw the whole story out as unbelievable were it not for the standing of the persons involved, the demonstration of the power that resulted from it, and the fact that this is just one step beyond examples we have already considered. It is, however, not far different from a series of experiences which I had in the spring of 1966, a series which changed my attitude about dreams from a sceptical 'perhaps' to a very positive acceptance. It is one thing to read about another's experiences, but they carry greater conviction when we know and trust the person involved. When they happen to us in ways we cannot doubt, we become witnesses of what we have seen and heard. So it was with me. I will tell the story in more detail, for without this experience this chapter, and possibly this book, would not have been written.

First, the original keys to my car were found on top of my notebook on a coffee table in our living room where they had not been fifteen minutes before. They had been lost six months previously and had presumably been carried to the dump. My wife and I tried every possible explanation, but found none. Finally I 'asked' for a confirmation if this were a real apport and had any significance. I am not sure whom I asked as I had no theory as to what happened or how — except that the keys were returned. This request was followed almost immediately by the finding of a copy of a German Iron Cross, the kind given for valor in France in 1914, under conditions just as strange and inexplicable. It had a lovely silver chain. Now I had a real mystery on my hands, for I had never taken apports seriously, thinking of them as like Jonah and the whale, or Washington and the cherry tree. But these were real apports which are in front of me as I type. This time I wrote in my prayer notebook, "What is the significance of the keys and the cross?"

This question was followed by a dream such as I never had before or since. First, two men, my physical father and my father in the ministry, George B. Cliff, appeared together. As far as I can remember I had never dreamed of either one. And in my dream I knew I was dreaming, and I asked the question, "Why have these men come to me?" The question should have been reversed as it was clear that I had come to them, not they to me. And immediately I heard a voice, spoken slowly and clearly, every word well modulated, entirely different from the vague impressionistic voices of most of my dreams. As the voice began I turned to look over my left shoulder to see if it was George Cliff, for that was where he was standing. Then I recognized that it was not his. As the words continued the figures faded, and I was aware only of the clear sound in my ears. These were the words:

"The subject is the essence of religion. The essence of religion is not in your beliefs or a system of theology. The essence of religion is not in an upright life or a system of ethics. The essence of religion is not in a church or a system of worship. But the essence of the *gospel* is the good news that God, as you know him in Jesus Christ, with all of his love, with all of his power, with all of his wisdom, and with all of his joy, is always and everywhere available to each and every person just as far as he or she is ready and willing to receive him. This is the essence of the gospel."

I am not here concerned with the content of the statement, although it is as fine a summary of the subject as I have heard, but with the sense that I was present in another realm. As the Apostle Paul said (2 Corinthians 12:2), "Whether in the body or out of the body I do not know," but it seemed, and still seems, more like the experience of John in Revelations 4:1: "And the first voice, which I heard speaking to me like a trumpet, said, 'Come up hither.' " The words were spoken to me with such authority that I could not doubt their reality, their truth, or their importance.

A dream out of my subconscious or the voice of an angel? I do not know; yet I can no longer doubt the possibility of angel voices speaking in dreams as recorded in both the Old and New Testaments. Such things may happen, because once they happened to me. Whether my own strange experiences with the keys and the cross were arranged by Clarence Matson and George Cliff to call attention to the dream I do not know. But I cannot separate the apports from the dream any more than Bishop Pike could separate the poltergeist happenings in his apartment at Cambridge from his son, Jim, who had recently committed suicide. As striking as the dream was, its significance might easily have slipped me if I had not previously recorded my question as to the meaning of the keys and the cross. The whole episode is a demonstration to me of the reality of the world of our beloved dead around us, who sometimes call us out of our physical bodies for some special reason.

Now we come to Swedenborg, the son of a Swedish bishop and a scientist and public official, who in 1743 at the age of fifty-five had a vision of which he later wrote: "I have been called to the holy office by the Lord himself . . . who opened my sight into the spiritual world, in which I have continued up to the present day [1769, when he was eighty-one]. From that time I began to print and publish the various arcana that were seen by me, or revealed to me, concerning Heaven and Hell, and the state of man after death." For the rest of his life he wrote volume after volume in simple Latin, publishing them at his own expense. Most of them deal primarily with the subject of this book. Whatever their source and technique they carry the 'feel' of authority of one who knew what he was talking about. At times he demonstrated a clairvoyance which sounded like the astral travel he claimed it was — though he never heard the term. While he lived in an age of strict eighteenth-century Lutheranism, the actual picture which he gives is largely in conformity with that given by twentieth-century mediumship. The most simple explanation is that what he claimed actually happened almost two centuries before such experiences and ideas became frequent, except that his came by astral projection whenever and wherever he desired instead of through mediumship.

Still another type of experience that bears many of the marks of astral travel is that of great inspiration. Handel has related how the windows of heaven were opened as he transcribed what he heard as the 'Hallelujah Chorus'. Mozart gives a more general account of his own inspiration as quoted by Catharine Crowe:

"When all goes well with me, when I am in a carriage, or walking, or even when I cannot sleep at night, the thoughts came streaming upon me most fluently; when or how is more than I can tell. What comes, I hum to myself as it proceeds. Then follow the counterpoint and clang of different instruments; and if I am not disturbed, my soul is fixed, and the thing grows greater, and broader, and clearer; and I have it all in my head, even when the piece is a long one; and I see it like a beautiful picture — not hearing the different parts in succession as they must be played, but the whole at once. That is the delight! The composing and the making is like a beautiful and vivid dream; but this hearing of it is best of all."[5]

Of all forms of travel from earth the most vital and fruitful is the mystic vision in which the unity and goodness of all existence is not merely perceived but experienced. It is known more by its fruits than by its logic. Among them is an awareness of the waiting world which takes one beyond all fear, and a joy indescribable and indestructible. Because ineffable, it often takes a symbolic form such as the Holy Grail, a wedding feast, or Pascal's fire. Yet it carries such a sense of reality, such a deep and wordless certainty that it seems during the vision, whether of an instant or days, that one is lifted above all earthly pleasure and bodily experience into another realm of heavenly knowledge and endless joy. Rarely was the Apostle Paul at a loss for words, but the experience of Paradise and the third heaven was so vivid and beyond reason that for once he was left speechless. But Francis Thompson caught it:

> O World invisible, we view thee;
> O world intangible, we touch thee;
> O world unknowable, we know thee
> Inapprehensible, we clutch thee!

Yet some do report back something of what they hear and experience. Some famous writers come to mind, Dante, Milton and Bunyan, as well as the Presbyter John who gave us the Apocalypse or Revelations. Each of these writes in magnificent symbolism and reveals a quality of inspiration at times that seems more of heaven than of earth. Must not also the great poet or preacher at times leave his prosaic body in order to bring the glory of eternity to the sons of men?

So travellers from earth are of many kinds, but our interest here is primarily in those who are called, whether in dreams or visions; in the great inspiration of musicians, artists, and writers; and in the mystics who themselves begin to share the quality not simply of the waiting world, but possibly of the eternal world or worlds beyond. Their reports are not at all inconsistent with the insights we have received at deathbeds and from the apparently dead, but they go much farther in emotional and spiritual depth. All through the ages there have been a few travellers from earth who have reported back their discoveries of exquisite beauty and ultimate truth by which the race has been advanced. Could we not also have here the secret of the great inventions which are milestones in human progress — the discovery of fire, the formation of languages, even the atom? Could it also be that the insights and skills of the great prophets, artists and mystics — Isaiah, Plato, Phidias, the Sufis, Handel — are but remainders, possibly *reminders*, of journeys out of the body and into life? It is a fascinating thought that all great inspirations are but dim reflections of the life which awaits us, and that they are often transmitted by travellers from earth, who have been called out for that purpose.

An intriguing theory that appears in many places and through many people is that we are entering a new age in history, an age marked not only by breathtaking progress in physical science, but also by corresponding advances in the arts of loving, living and working together as the human race moves forward toward a world society. One aspect of this is an increase in the number of persons with unusual spiritual and psychic gifts. This has been highlighted for me by four close personal contacts with different individuals, all of whom are involved in some form of astral travel out of this world. Two of them in everyday life are housewives and mothers; yet in their secret thoughts they roam the universe, at home in two worlds at one time. The other two are both electronic engineers engaged in advanced research, but their greatest thrills are in their daily contacts with the unseen world. The question that keeps bobbing up in my mind is, have these four been sent to me to confirm my faith and to guide my thinking as I write? Or have there always been many such persons around, but I was not ready to know and accept them? In either case my courage has been increased and my thinking clarified by them.

Always the human race has had its pioneers who have lived ahead of their times, explored regions beyond those yet occupied, and reported back their findings to the larger numbers who ultimately would follow. Even more significant than the physical exploration of the moon are those travellers into life who not only describe the nature of the life awaiting us all, but who become samples of the heavenly life while living among men. Their reports all go to confirm and clarify the more shadowy pictures we get from the dying and the pseudo-dead.

6 The Dead Report

The dead report back? "But they don't!" Many times my face is red as I think of sermons that I once preached in my ignorance. Of course I had the scripture, most of it from the Old Testament. My professors and teachers in seminary may not have been too sure about heaven, but they all agreed there was no back-talk from the grave. So did the theologians and biblical commentators. And so did our real authority, the Great God Science. Even commonsense supported this viewpoint. I had everything but the truth! And the facts!

It was on an afternoon late in June of 1958 that I had my first experience with Arthur Ford. How clearly I remember! About twenty of us met in a hotel room in Hollywood. Most of us had no real idea what to expect, even though we had heard him speak at a Spiritual Frontiers Fellowship seminar the day before, and had read his autobiography *Nothing So Strange*.[1] The place was crowded and I was sitting on the floor, not sure whether I was betraying my calling as a Protestant minister, or had allowed myself to be taken in by a medieval charlatan in modern garb. I can still remember the queer feeling in the pit of my stomach. It never occurred to me to take notes. I was the only preacher present. It was a typical Ford sitting, but for me it was an introduction into a new world.

To my surprise there was nothing dark or mysterious. Ford explained that Fletcher, whom he had known slightly in boyhood, was his master of ceremonies "on the other side", using the medium's voice, and sometimes his hands. He went on to explain that there were always a great number of friends and relatives present hoping to make contact with those they knew still in their physical bodies. Fletcher decided who should have the floor, speaking for them at first and making sure that both parties knew and recognized each other. If a name was given that seemed to be for one of us, that person should reply. When there was mutual recognition, conversation continued naturally as far as possible. He explained that in the next life speech is not by sound, but by ideas, often in terms of symbols, so it was often very difficult to get names at first. We were to be as natural as we could and were perfectly free to ask questions.

Then Ford tied a sash around his head, apparently only to keep out the light so that he could go into trance. He settled back comfortably in an over-stuffed chair and began to breathe deeply. In several minutes he began to mumble as though he were talking in his sleep, but soon his voice cleared and we heard him say that he was Fletcher, and that a lot of our friends were there wanting to talk with us. In most cases he would give a name and ask if somebody present recognized it. Several times somebody said they had a friend by the name given, but Fletcher was very positive in his identifications and would not accept the wrong person. Often it was not a close relative, but someone known years ago and recalled with difficulty. Several times there was no memory of the facts cited, and the person involved was told to check on them.

There were several names which I tried to claim, but each one proved to be for somebody else. Finally Ford, or Fletcher using Ford's body, pointed down to me sitting on the floor almost at his feet, and said, "You're a preacher, aren't you?" I nodded and said that I was. He continued, "There's a Catholic priest here, Father McManus, who says he knew you in Alaska. Do you remember him?"

"No, I can't seem to recall him." (I was a pastor in Alaska at Ketchikan all during the war.)

"Well, he knows you well. He was a chaplain, and you used to hold services for him. Later he flew out to the Aleutians and was drowned in a plane accident." I must have been too rattled to think, but I still could not recall him. (Later I did remember that I had conducted Protestant services for Father McManus who was the only chaplain on Annette Island. The invitations had stopped, and I had completely forgotten the matter.)

The voice went on, "There is a friend of his here whose name I can't quite get — Bax — Bax — Bruce Bax. He says he was your superior officer." Of course I knew Bishop Bruce Baxter, a good bishop and a wonderful personal friend. "He says his headquarters were at Portland." (Correct.)

From here on the conversation continued as though there were no intermediaries between Bruce and myself. He went on to explain that he had taken it upon himself to arrange for my new appointment, and that there are certain things that I should do there, primarily as part of my training for work in the future. It so happened that I had been appointed just two days before to a new job as an associate pastor in California, a position which I had said I would not take. A series of coincidences which my wife called "God incidences" finally led me to accept it. Time proved that the appointment was certainly right. We would not have missed those years for anything.

This experience was something wholly new to me and left me almost trembling. Could it be that the dead are not only alive and still interested in us, but in some cases are able to manipulate events with a wisdom and power beyond anything I had been able to conceive possible? After almost eleven years I am still sure that there were a number of factors in that appointment which were inexplicable in any logical way. I find myself still wondering and usually believing that my former friend was continuing to exercise power as a bishop to make sure that we were sent where we belonged. It was an experience both humbling and exalting, as well as exciting, and I have never been quite the same since that afternoon in Hollywood.

I had read many books and believed in a rather vague way, but now it had happened to me! In a way almost beyond doubt I know that at least some of the dead live; they care about me, and they are able to help! I have to say almost beyond doubt because it is still possible to say that telepathy was involved in the sitting, or that Ford had researched my past and present situations. However, any sober analysis gives such odds against either explanation that I would have to be indeed gullible to accept either of them. Then when the added fact that most of the others in the room had equally amazing experiences is considered, it becomes completely preposterous to think that the session was anything else than was claimed, that is, brief chats of old friends and relatives now living in two different worlds. Moreover, Ford had no way of knowing who was coming in advance, and most of them he had never met until just before he went into trance.

As I continued to think about the session I began to wonder about some of the things I had both believed and preached. Could it be that our Roman Catholic friends are right not only in praying for the dead, but also in praying to the saints? The former I have long believed in, and sometimes practised; but since that afternoon I have often given fervent thanks to (as well as for) Bruce Baxter, still my friend and uncanonized Protestant saint.

Later I began to wonder about the differences between my lackadaisical attitude toward the stories I had read and heard about others and my own intense feelings about what had happened to me with Ford in Hollywood. I had read many books and a few friends had recounted their own personal experiences, but I continued to think and preach as before, although sometimes raising questions privately and even in small groups. But no longer so! My feelings had completely changed, although my experience was no more evidential than that of ten thousand others — or of the twenty who were with me in Hollywood. I now read and listen to the tales of others with a different interest and more under-standing. I have been there! So also is it in many other fields. In listening to the television news recently I was much relieved to learn that a disastrous fire in which lives were lost was not in California, but in an eastern city — as if the tragedy were any less for being far away.

This is the reason why I am here dealing almost entirely with my own experiences. They are real and convincing to me, and I feel there is a better chance of bringing not mere agreement, but emotional acceptance to the reader if I can say, "This is what I saw, and experienced, and know." When I finally describe some details of the waiting world, many other sources will be quoted which I now trust not only because of their intrinsic value or because many clear-thinking writers believe them, but because I myself first investigated and became convinced that this strange phenomenon is often as trustworthy as the results in any other field of advanced human research. It is obvious that few of my stories in earlier chapters could be personal. I have not yet died, or nearly so; nor have I seen many ghosts. But here I can tell what it was I saw and heard that finally convinced me.

Eight years after my first experience with Arthur Ford in Hollywood, my wife and I had a private sitting with him near Philadelphia, and Baxter again came through, apparently trying to correct what he had decided was an unfair judgement of a nationally known colleague. The statements originally made during a West Coast seance had been so harsh that those present agreed before they left the room never to repeat them. When I commented on his change of mind the Bishop (although he did not use that term of himself) insisted that his present judgement was correct, and asked me to carry the message to his former colleague, which I did. From this I would judge that it is possible to sin and repent even after we have left our physical bodies.

At this same session there were four other voices each claiming to be ministerial friends and having interesting comments. Of course I have no way of being sure they were actually the persons the voice coming through the sleeping Ford claimed them to be; yet in each case they were very much in character, and the identification seemed valid as far as I could judge. To think otherwise requires greater skill than I can conceive Ford as having. Each of these four gave interesting hints about the world beyond, so I will summarize them briefly on the assumption that they were indeed the surviving personalities of the men they claimed to be.

The first was Dudley Barr, whom I could not recall at all at first. He insisted that he organized a church where I later preached, and that I had conducted his funeral. After returning home I checked my records and discovered that he was indeed the first pastor of the Broadway church in Glendale, and that I had assisted at his funeral at Forest Lawn in 1958. He went on to say that I was the only preacher with whom he could hope to communicate, and that he had been trying for a long time. This was seven years after his death. I had never actually known him except very incidentally at conference, and he really had nothing to say, but wanted to talk — like many a preacher I have known. He sounded very lonely.

It often seems that persons coming into the next life with strong convictions and definite expectations are much confused when they find a world far different from the one they had anticipated. This has nothing to do with their character, their faith, or their ultimate goal, only with the fact that they are so rigid in their hopes that they find it impossible for a while to grasp the greater glory of what God has prepared for them. Thus it was in the New Testament when the Pharisees found it hard to appreciate Jesus when he ate with publicans and sinners (see Matthew 9:11-13). They could not imagine God as good as Jesus claimed.

Next was Roy Burkhart who had been scheduled to be the president of Spiritual Frontiers Fellowship at the time of his sudden death. He had come through another medium, Martin Strauch of Detroit, the preceding November, when a small group of us were trying to work out a future programme for Spiritual Frontiers Fellowship. As we sat in the circle with the medium, Roy, fully in character, took the very active part in the discussion which he would have had he been physically present as our president. Now here he was again ready with advice and philosophy. He did not waste time proving his identity, but simply continued from where he had left off in Detroit. He approved of the way we had carried out some of our assignments, but spoke accurately and disparagingly about a book I had started, and gave me some personal advice about my activities in the years ahead. He also spoke very sharply of preachers who read the Bible from the pulpit and then tell the people it is not true. He insisted that there was no hope for the church unless the Holy Spirit is recognized as still functioning and guiding. There was much more, all in the spirit of the Roy Burkhart some of us had known. Yet there was a sparkle missing.

A third voice, a preacher as I later learned, began without introduction to congratulate my wife and me on our son, and to say how much his sons would enjoy getting acquainted with him. This meant nothing to me, and I asked who he was. He gave the name of Zabriskie. I later learned that a Zabriskie had been Dean of the Virginia Theological Seminary where our son was hoping to study, and that he had two sons in the Episcopal priesthood in that area. This was especially interesting to me as here was a man I had never heard of who knew what was being planned although he did not know that our son's plans would change, and that he would stay on the West Coast.

The same name appears in the former Bishop Pike's book *The Other Side,*[2] in the sitting of Pike with Ford which was broadcast over the Canadian Broadcasting System. So Dean Zabriskie came through Fletcher and Ford to me in 1965 and to Pike in 1967. Apparently the old Dean is still around and much interested in his lovely seminary across the river from Washington. Although Ford was involved each time he surely could not have known about Bishop Pike's involvement with Zabriskie, nor my interest in the seminary our son was planning to attend. The explanation must be in Zabriskie himself with Ford being simply the transmitter, as he claimed to be.

A fourth voice urged us to put younger men like Father Rauscher, an Episcopal rector in New Jersey who was also mentioned to Pike by an English medium, in places of leadership (presumably in Spiritual Frontiers Fellowship). Then, apparently realizing that I was no longer young, he went on to say that I was still young in spirit, and "that is why you are always in trouble". That was even worse, so he then said how he had often been in hot water because he always spoke out on so many issues. He had not bothered to give his name, but when I asked it he said without hesitation, "Bob Shuler." I expressed surprise that he had died, and he replied that I was thinking about his son (Bob Shuler, Jr). Later I checked and learned that Bob Shuler, Sr, for many years a controversial ecclesiastical and political figure in southern California, was in a coma for quite some time before his death which took place weeks after this apparent appearance through Ford in the east.

What can we make of this? Nobody was farther from my

mind than Bob Shuler, Sr. We had never been intimate although he had preached for me, and we had shared in funeral services. Yet he appeared in character even in assuming that I would know him. If Ford was trying to cheat he would hardly have chosen a man who was not yet dead, though close to it. Could it be that the spirit of a man sometimes leaves his body and wanders over the earth (as was suggested in Chapter II)? I do not know, but it is at least an interesting possibility.

What was I to make of these experiences with mediums, and of others like them? At home, in college and at seminary I had been warned to keep away from all such matters. In my boyhood home it was not a matter of actual rules any more than drunkenness, or immorality or swearing. All I knew was that Matsons had nothing to do with them, and this I accepted as naturally as my country or the color of my skin. Ghosts, fortune tellers, mediums and the devil had no real existence as far as we were concerned. This was much more effective than denunciation, because nobody kicks a dead dog or beats the air to prove his strength.

College and seminary reinforced this assumption and erected intellectual and emotional walls around me as protection from contact with anything and everything in this field. (The compilers of my desk dictionary[3] must have had this same wall around them as it does not even include the word 'mediumship'.) I did vaguely remember, however, one seminary lecture on the origins of prophecy in the Old Testament which suggested that it began with religious ecstasy. Surely enough, when I turned to the earliest stories of prophecy in Numbers 11:25-26 and 1 Samuel 10:5-6, the descriptions sound like a trance during which the spirit of the Lord is interpreted as speaking. King Saul when so possessed at one time by an evil spirit from God tried to kill David, and a little later lay naked a day and a night as he prophesied (1 Samuel 18:10-11 and 19:24). This could be described either as trance mediumship or as prophecy "before it was converted". It is this sort of thing that the Old Testament law condemns so strongly, not only among the Hebrews but among their pagan neighbors. Yet when cleansed of its pagan and primitive aspects it became the basis for Hebrew prophecy, simply a succession of men who had so come under the spell of God that they could rightly say "Thus saith the Lord!"

The German Catholic priest, Johannes Greber, was told at great length by the spirits who spoke to him through a fifteen-year-old boy, that the Old Testament schools of the prophets were schools of mediumship; and that the prophecies were originally given in trance or semi-trance. I know of no other hypothesis which so adequately explains the great prophets of ancient Israel both in their ethical qualities and their vision of the future. Their poetic rhythmic form is also common in trance. The great prophets were possessed or entranced by divine spirits just as Peter and Paul were (Acts 10:9-15 and 22:17-21). The same may be said of those who speak in strange tongues or ecstasies, as well as those who interpret for them (1 Corinthians 14:2-33). Whether it is God or angel messengers makes no difference. But, as both Testaments make abundantly clear, there are not only good, but also evil spirits who seek to possess and to deceive. The evil are warned against and are to be cast out (Matthew 10:1, 8), while the good are to be encouraged and obeyed.

In "trying the spirits" I began to read the books mentioned in the Appendix and many others like them. There I also ran into all the types of evidence already mentioned, though the majority dealt with mediumship in one way or other. The quality was often very poor; the writers were gullible, accepting as gospel truth every word purporting to have come through mediums or spirit guides. Others were highly imaginative and symbolic, embroidering their narratives with fanciful details beyond any rational consideration. Yet here they have good authority in the books of Daniel and Revelation which surpass most of them in symbolic descriptions. Much of it was so childish that it was sickening, and almost turned me away from the whole field. A great deal of it was idle gossip and chitchat. One even talked of smoking cigars! For many years I felt that Halford Luccock was wise in dropping the whole subject with the remark that it was inconceivable that the next life was so utterly stupid. Only because my own experience was so persuasive did I persist until I finally learned what I believe are the facts. At last the pieces began to fall into place like a jigsaw puzzle.

But there were also many writers whose words carried a ring of truth. Some had great difficulty in accepting what the evidence indicated to be the truth, but finally felt compelled to give their witness. Among them were scientists and scholars who started out to expose mediumship as both irrational and fraudulent, but were converted to its veracity and significance. They came as scoffers, but remained to pray. Some became officers or investigators for the British or American Society for Psychical Research, and spent years attempting to uncover fraud and to present alternative theories before coming to the inescapable conclusion that in some cases, at least, the dead do return and speak. Their reports fill many volumes. I found no person who with honest and open mind carefully investigated the evidence, but who was not more or less convinced, often grudgingly and reluctantly. But I also found many, both scientists and theologians, who continued to attack without examining the facts. I remember, for example, a more candid than usual attack in a psychological journal on the work of Dr J. B. Rhine of Duke University. The writer said that in any other field one-tenth of the evidence that Rhine presented would be adequate to substantiate his thesis; but in the absence of a theory explaining how it could be true (linkage: see Chapter XII), ten times the evidence would not persuade him to examine the subject. That may well be an expression of human nature facing a revolutionary change, but it is certainly not scientific or rational when considering the central questions of the nature and destiny of each one of us.

Yet I found the poor books almost as signicifant on the whole as the reports of the Societies for Psychical Research and such men as J. B. Rhine, Raynor Johnson, Frederic Myers, Leslie Weatherhead, or Alson Smith. As suggested previously, in all they carry a tremendous weight by their wide agreements in spite of triteness, gullibility and fancifulness. When allowance is made for these qualities and the limitations of the writers, it was clear that they agree on eighty per cent of the material I shall present as a fair description of the new world waiting for all who seriously read this book. The vocabulary, interpretations and reasoning of a college professor and a kindergarten child may differ greatly, but on basic questions of fact they will agree. More than that, a child's statement of what did happen is of far more value than a professor's theory of what cannot. My friend Chris was five years old and spent many hours playing with what his grandparents called a spirit playmate. Then the family cat began to show signs of great and inexplicable fear which the boy explained as the cat's startling discovery of the playmate and recognition of him as an enemy. Under some conditions even a cat may be a witness! There are many familiar stories of dogs not only howling when a spirit leaves the body, but of recognizing friends and enemies in the spirit world.

Before we conclude this chapter on mediumship it is necessary to notice some of its many varieties, and to see the unity between them. One definition of 'medium' is a "person serving, or conceived as serving, as an instrument for the manifestation of another personality, or of some other alleged supernatural agency". It may be either in complete or partial trance, or in full consciousness. In the latter case the medium claims to stand aside and report either by voice or pen what is taking place, but without controlling it. It is easier for those watching to accept the phenomena as genuine when the medium is in full trance, but the validity of the experience and the value of the material which comes through are apparently not affected by the depth of the trance. In most cases it is similar to dreams in that there is little or no residue of memory left for long afterward. Yet it does seem in some cases that the material is influenced or directed by the subconscious of the medium. Arthur Ford has told me, for example, that he is sure that this 'coloring' occurs at times even though he is in complete trance. That could be true for the first part of the Shuler material.

Many studies also seem to indicate that the character of the spirit or entity using some part of the medium's body has to be compatible with the character of the medium himself. A clean-minded and spiritual person is protected from mischievous and deceiving spirits as a purely curious person is not. Only a low or weak minded person, regardless of outward appearances, can be possessed by an evil spirit. There has to be a meshing of gears, a concurrence of desire, or at least acquiescence, before there can be any takeover. This has nothing to do with the intellectual content of what may come through, but only with its character. Thus the prophets of Israel, being God-dedicated and directed men, as well as trained in the techniques of trance, could be used to present revelations of divine character and purpose beyond anything previously grasped by the race.

The most common forms of mediumship involve either the vocal cords for speaking or the hands for automatic writing. I have had no experience with any who claim to create the actual voices through trumpets or materializations with ectoplasm. Whether genuine or not, they are for the curious and gullible; nor do I know of their making any contribution to our knowledge of the next world. Other types, according to our dictionary definition, would include various ways of by-passing the critical conscious mind such as the ouija board, the pendulum and crystal ball, glossolalia and demon possession, but, again, rarely do they add anything to our study and so do not come within the limits of this book. The same could be said of voice phenomena on radio and tapes.

Mediumship spells out in much greater detail and perhaps accuracy a picture of the waiting world to which our earlier chapters on the Bible, science, deathbed scenes, apparitions and Lazarus experiences can only point in a partial and shadowy way. A bit more is learned from travellers from earth like Swedenborg, but mediumship is the crown which gives confirmation and clarity to all the rest. None of them, not even the Bible, could carry conviction to the modern mind standing by itself. But when all are taken together they portray a world of life and hope which men of integrity and intelligence may accept and expect. When this picture becomes a faith it may well prove to be an essential factor leading to a new heaven on earth — at least in the fast-approaching twenty-first century.

7 The Thrill of Dying

Through Hades to Paradise in Three Days

Now we come to the real question: can we take these reports of mediums and astral travellers as actual and dependable descriptions of the experiences all of us will be having sooner or later? Or are they fairy tales no more valid than Santa Claus or Jack-in-the-Beanstalk? Traditional descriptions of heaven and hell were once used, like a year around Santa Claus, to keep us on the straight and narrow path, although I cannot recall they ever had any effect on my behavior. Perhaps for some they did.

But these stories, many of which are very detailed, confirmed by reputable witnesses, from all cultures, centuries and continents, cannot be lightly dismissed when we take seriously the four "Watchmen of Science" (discussed in Chapter XI). If we are to know the truth about the basic matters of human destiny — and in the long run no other questions are of greater importance — we must carefully consider the picture of life they present. Their basic coherence and unity point toward a world of reality unknown to physical science.

I shall now attempt to construct a picture of such a world, and to test that picture by the canons of scientific thought. This is one way that progress has always been made. The world locks flat, but the evidence which Columbus (and the ancient Greeks) uncovered needs a sphere for explanation. Columbus thought that he had proved it by sailing west and finding the Indies, but Magellan circled the globe as the final confirmation. So also is it with evolution, relativity and every step in science and invention. When the kinds of evidence presented in the last five chapters are fitted together they form a consistent picture of the waiting world, which can then be tested by other evidence. Ultimately it must be confirmed, amplified and corrected. Or it may be replaced by an utterly different concept, as have ancient theories of disease and astronomy. In the meantime we do the best we can with the evidence at our disposal — just as Columbus and Einstein did.

The most complete study of the material we are considering from a research angle has been done by Dr Robert Crookall, an English geologist.[1] Dr Crookall analyzed thousands of psychic experiences and communications, and discovered that they form a pattern largely in conformity with the evidence presented in previous chapters. In the absence of contrary testimony of equal validity, logic compels us to accept some such description as a working hypothesis. The outline here presented is largely a simplified adaptation of his conclusions together with some confirmatory material from other sources.

In a more personal and popular way this material may be considered to be a travel guide to a journey we all are to take. Any ocean voyage has its disadvantages, seasickness, for example, but they are never mentioned in travel agents' brochures. Here we will describe the voyage called death, and later the country where all of us presumably will be settling. Then, as fair warning to the traveller, I shall discuss the nature and reality of hell and how to avoid it.

Before we begin our imaginary journey we need to come to some understanding about vocabulary. A leading psychiatrist has said that we are living in a new Tower of Babel because the same terms are used with many varied meanings, and similar experiences are described by a great variety of overlapping expressions. Note that Swedenborg's 'heaven', Myer's 'plane of illusion', Stewart Edwart White's 'unobstructed universe'[2], and Crookall's 'paradise' all refer to the same thing. This could also be what Jesus promised to the thief on the cross, "This day thou shalt be with me in paradise."

Some of the other terms with varied and overlapping meanings are 'personality', 'astral,' 'etheric,' 'spiritual,' 'soul,' 'Hades,' 'heaven,' 'hell,' and 'death'. Here I will generally follow Crookall's terminology. When making direct quotations in which these and similar words are used in a different sense I will follow with a parenthesis enclosing my word. Perhaps thus we can get down from our Tower of Babel and understand each other.

The world beyond, at least in its aspects immediately after this life, may be conveniently divided, like ancient Gaul, into three parts. We will call them by the old and familiar names of Hades, paradise and heaven. These are successive planes of existence referred to already in a variety of ways. Their validity will be considered again later, but for the time being we may assume that the preponderance of our evidence is trustworthy, and simply try to get as clear a picture as is possible under the circumstances. Read it as science fiction, if necessary, but try to grasp it as an intriguing picture of the world as God may have made it. *It just might be true!*

But first a little about the structure of personality itself. Living in a day of travel to the moon this will be easier to grasp than ever before. We know there are many kinds of energy waves in space; although we perceive only a small part of them as light and heat, they carry on many functions without interfering with each other. We are also aware, at least in theory, that modern astronomy has opened up new realms of speculation involving millions of galaxies billions of light years away. And likewise, atomic physics reveals whirling worlds of the infinitely small beyond our power to measure, yet required by the evidence of the laboratory. In this new world disclosed to us by science there is plenty of room for the non-physical realities implied by our evidence.

Let us begin by postulating several realms of being occupying the same space, each of them existing independently and with its own density or vibratory rate, just as there may be many telephone conversations carried over one wire, or television programs in the same room. One of these realms is the familiar physical world of matter and light together with all that functions in it. This is the world of science that we know and can measure. Now we assume that there is another world of reality (perhaps more than one) with its own laws and phenomena. What these are we can only dimly surmise as we consider the kind of material we have been discussing. These two worlds apparently come together in living creatures — the one that we know physically and the other through extra-sensory perception and related phenomena.

The next step is to describe an individual person in terms of these two realms of existence. There are at least two bodies. One of them we can see and weigh, and has all the physical capacities we know so well. It is a temporary and dying body, made and kept alive by the spirit body in which consciousness and reason abide, and which survives the change called death. The real person or soul centres in the spirit body, and only temporarily uses and expresses itself through the physical body which is its creation and shadow.

The evidence for the existence and nature of this body is found in many of the phenomena already discussed, as well as the assumptions of causation and linkage. There must be such bodies just as there have to be atoms and molecules, although in neither case do we have instruments for observing them. Their footprints move across the pages of every life even though we have been blind to both their presence and meaning.

While these two bodies are normally alike in size and shape, we are conscious only when they occupy the same space and the spirit functions through the physical brain and nervous system. There seems to be a sheath, a unifying double, or a 'vehicle of vitality' (as Crookall calls it) which unites them. There are times when these bodies are more or less separated from each other and then we are unconscious, as during sleep, under drugs, or in trance. When so separated the vehicle of vitality functions as the silver cord (see Ecclesiastes 12:6) variously described as a spider web, an elastic cable or string, a ribbon or thread of light, or a pipeline in reports of astral travel. It is capable of being indefinitely stretched and is usually connected at the solar plexus or at the base of the brain. Only when this cord is cut or broken so that the spirit body cannot return to the physical, do the processes of decay set in.

We now see that there may be two definitions of death, both quite different from the traditional ones dealing with the cessation of the heartbeat and other vital processes.

Death may be considered as an extensive period, often thought of in terms of three days, beginning either when the soul becomes aware of the non-physical world, as in deathbed scenes, or loses consciousness. The death process ends when the soul consciousness awakes to paradise conditions. This process may be reversible at any time before the cord is broken. When this process is reversed we have what Crookall calls 'pseudo-death' and the phenomenon of so-called astral travel.

The second definition is much simpler. Death is permanent separation of the physical and soul bodies and takes place when the cord is cut. However, that may be at any stage of the period, sometimes instantly, as in the case of violent death, but more normally somewhat later. The silver cord is comparable to the umbilical cord without which no life can be maintained in an unborn baby. The cutting or destruction of one marks the new birth into the physical world, and the other into the spirit world.

Just as there are many differences in the human birth process, so also is there even greater variety in the next birth, which men call death. Caesarean section in human birth is comparable to forced or violent death, for example. Other variations are caused by the age, health and spiritual development of the soul. However, there is one great difference between physical and soul birth. The human physical baby may die, but never the soul — even of an unborn baby. All of us are sentenced not only to physical death, but also to the life of the next world. There is no escape and there is no hiding place. Here we shall deal primarily with average and fairly good people, the kind who will generally be reading this book. For these death takes place normally when the physical body is so weakened by age, disease, or accident that it can no longer be maintained as a suitable instrument of the soul.

What may we expect both for ourselves and our friends?

Firstly, death is painless and pleasant! Practically all witnesses agree on this. No matter how disagreeable the preliminaries may be, as in some forms of cancer or typhoid, actual death is easy and usually welcome.

In the book *Many Lifetimes* by Denys Kelsey and Joan

Grant, there is the story of the death of their friend Ray. Dr Kelsey, a psychiatrist with some psychic ability, was able to make a contact with her a few days later. The words came quickly: "What fun it is to die! Dying is not at all solemn . . . There is not even the sadness I expected at being physically parted. Tell them there is no loneliness here, and so much joy to share."[3]

Karlis Osis in his studies,[4] has confirmed the ease and often the elation with which terminal patients approach the end. Crookall's reports, coming through scores of mediums, are in complete agreement at this point. Myers, writing through Geraldine Cummins,[5] says, "The average man or woman when he or she is dying suffers no pain. They have become so dissevered already from the body that when the flesh seems to be in agony the actual soul merely feels very drowsy . . . So grieve not for the apparent agony of the dying, rejoice because they are already freed . . ."

Sometimes this departure from the body may take place days or weeks before final death as in the case of Bob Shuler, Sr, who came to me through Arthur Ford. This could be an example of astral projection, as I have no way of knowing whether he was still returning to the body or not, and I doubt if he knew. He gave no sign of it.

When death comes suddenly or violently it seems to be equally painless. Crookall gives numerous examples both of those who have died and reported through mediums, and of astral projectors, indicating that an instant before a blow from a fall or accident the conscious entity is shocked out of the physical body and so feels nothing. Thus, David Livingstone, telling of being attacked by a lion, said, "He shook me like a terrier does a rat. It caused a sort of dreaminess in which there was no sense of pain or feeling of terror, although I was conscious of all that happened."[6] Most of us have had the experience in accidents of not being aware we were hurt until later. It is apparently the same when the injuries are serious enough to cause death. Moreover, from all reports I have read, death by freezing or drowning is also very comfortable and peaceful once it is accepted as inevitable.

The only exceptions I have been able to find are of some who anticipated great pain and thus found and remembered it. The one specific case which I recall was of a woman beheaded during the French Revolution, and who reported a century and a half later through a medium that it was excruciating. This may be the exception that proves the rule, and could be a fair warning not to die by that form of execution. Or, more likely, her expectation was so much greater than her vague memory of the event itself that she reported only the fearful death she anticipated through imagination, not what actually happened. All forms are painless and without fear when the actual moment comes. A line from an old English poem by William Collins has a point here: "The brave die but once, but the coward many times."

It should be pointed out, however, that the process of returning to the body is often fraught with fear and pain — that is, for those who are forced to come back (as described in Chapter III). When Arthur Ford, for example, was supposed to be dying in a hospital in Coral Gables, Florida, he was consciously visiting the next realm where he was judged not to have finished his job in the body, and so was ordered to return. He says, "At the doorway of return I balked like a spoiled child in a tantrum — braced my feet and fought against going. There was a sudden sense of hurtling through space, and I found myself looking into the face of a nurse."[7]

Crookall quotes Leslie Grant Scott[8]: "Dying is really not such a terrifying experience. I died and came back. I found death one of the easiest things in life, but not the returning; that was difficult and full of fear." Could it be that just as the birth of a baby is fraught with difficulty and pain so also is the much rarer return of a spirit to its physical body?

Secondly, we are usually met by a reception committee. It is necessary only to refer back to the stories related in Chapter II and to note that, according to Dr Osis, almost 40 per cent of the 3,500 persons who were observed as fully conscious at the time of death saw visions of recognized persons or religious figures.[9] It is significant also that in the cases checked on by Dr Osis none of those without religious faith or belief in immortality had visions either of persons or of scenes of beauty. The reasons for this will become evident when we discuss hell.

As for the greater number who were *not* reported as having

had such an experience, it could well be that many of them did have them, but were not able to communicate the fact. My father-in-law simply raised his two arms and was gone. It is possible that with others who were already unconscious because the spirit body had become separated from the earthly one, the vision came but there was no possibility of communicating it.

Another limiting factor is found in those who did not believe, were of low spiritual development, or had no warning of impending death. None of these would have been thinking about friends who had preceded them in death. This seems to be the way the 'committee' is alerted to the arrival of their beloved one. If I fail to notify friends or relatives that I am arriving at an airport, naturally they will not be on hand to greet me; but I will find somebody who can give me information and get me on my way. Of course, if I am too proud to ask, too stubborn to admit that I need help, or insist that I cannot be at the airport, I will be left to wallow in my misery.

It is true in this life, and all the evidence seems to say that it will be the same in the next, and that is that I will find myself lost in wanderings between dreams which are often more like nightmares. But anyone curious enough to have read thus far need have no worries. There will be friends to show you the ropes, or especially delegated spirit guides to help you on your way. Only an attitude of absolute rejection or know-it-all-ness casts a fog over one's spirit eyes. Even then, whenever help is called for, it is given.

Thirdly, there is often a rapid review of the life like a movie in reverse. Every detail of the past from death back to infancy is seen, sometimes in an instant, and all of it with startling clarity. Much that was completely forgotten is suddenly recaptured. The majority of these reports come from people who thought they were going to be killed in a crash or drowned, but who were finally saved. For example, Charles Hampton, a Liberal Catholic, tells about the editor of a newspaper in Butte, Montana, who claimed that he fell from an apple tree at the age of nine, and that before he struck the ground there flashed through his mind everything that had ever happened to him in his brief life.[10] Crookall has got together about thirty such incidences in *The Supreme Adventure*.[11] It is not quite clear whether this is a universal experience, or more often limited to those on the verge of violent death, although, again, Crookall lists a few similar cases coming through mediums.[12]

This quick survey is not a judgement, but a quick review without emotion. We are neither elated by the good nor cast down by the evil in our lives. The judgement comes only when we are ready for it, and will be discussed later. Gloria Lee, however, who passed over at the end of a two-month fast, had an immediate experience of a very painful judgement, but this seems to be an exception rather than the rule. She was an advanced soul and was probably ready for it far earlier than most of us.

Fourthly, we enter into the sleep of Hades. This may not be a sleep at all, as in cases of violent death when the cord is cut at the same time. Just as with earth sleep, its nature varies greatly. With some it is dreamless, so no report is possible. Sometimes there may be nightmares and dreams interspersed with periods of drowsy wakefulness or semi-consciousness. It is never in any way a time of pain or punishment, but of readjustment before the transition is completed.

The report made by Frederic Myers through Geraldine Cummins well sums up what the average person who reads this may expect.[13]

"Pray do not conjure up unpleasant associations with Hades. I died in Italy, a land that I loved, and I was very weary at the time of my passing. For me, Hades was a place of rest, a place of half-lights and drowsy peace. As a man wins strength from a long deep sleep, so did I gather that spiritual and intellectual force I needed during the time I abode in Hades. According to his nature and makeup every traveller from the earth is affected in a different or varying manner by this place on the frontiers of two lives, on the borders of two worlds."

In cases of sudden death from accident or in battle where there is no forewarning and the silver cord or lifeline is severed at the same time, there is no sleep, except perhaps for a momentary blackout. There may be no realization of death. Often soldiers go on fighting and cannot understand why their comrades do not respond to them. Only when they see their own dead bodies, or recognize others whom they know to have been killed, do they realise that this is death. Sometimes they discover that physical objects they can still see are no longer obstacles but can be passed through. Remember (see Chapter III) the two medical doctors, A. S. Wiltse and George Ritchie, who died and were restored. In our everyday world the physical body is solid and heavy while the spirit is ghostly, no more than the wind. In Hades the opposite is true. Seeing this, the half-born spirit finally understands that he is dead. Or he may be told by spirit helpers, if he is willing to learn. They are always on the lookout for lost souls who have not warned their friends and relatives by thoughts of them preceding death, and who need to be rescued and put in touch with a reception committee.

The Hades period, or Sheol in the Old Testament, was all that was known of the next world by many primitive peoples, and more than is recognized by many in our so-called civilized world. There is little that is attractive about this life, if life it can be called. No wonder that among the Jews of Jesus' day it had given way to the absolute extinction of the Sadducees or to the Persian theory of death and resurrection adopted by the Pharisees. Another form of escape from the idea of Hades is the extinction of desire in Nirvana, which is the goal of Buddhism. But Hades is not the end of our story, only a pause for adjusting to new conditions, and not all bad.

While the traditional end of the Hades period comes in three days, much evidence indicates that there are earth-bound souls who are so emotionally tied to earth that they remain there indefinitely. As Myers says of them:[14]

"If (a dead man) passes through the gates of death bearing with him a passionate love of material possessions, he will, even after a fleeting glimpse of his discarnate kindred, tenaciously hold to the belief that he is still a man of flesh and blood, wandering, perhaps on the hills in a mist, but still filled with the life of earth. He will passionately seek for his house, his money, or whatever is his particular treasure, in the dark days beyond death."

There are others, too involved in passionate love or crime,

possibly suicides, and some perhaps so stubbornly materialistic they will not accept the fact of the next life, who as souls in prison need our prayers and love. Remember that Jesus came to save them, too (1 Peter 3:20). These are barely mentioned here to complete our picture, not to describe the experience. They are the reality behind many ghost stories, however.

Fifthly, the physical and soul bodies are separated. This is a three-stage affair, but because we are unconscious of it, although not of its consequences, they can be considered together. The net result is that we are freed from the ties of earth and move into, or awake in, paradise. Viewed from the outside it could be described in terms of the vision of Diane Kennedy Pike[15] who saw her husband leaving his body three days after he was supposed to have died, and rising to a higher realm where he was welcomed by a great crowd of friends.

Perhaps a simple diagram will help if we do not take it too literally. The three circles from greater to smaller represent the physical body, the vehicle of vitality or unifying body, and the spirit body. 'S' stands for the soul or centre of consciousness.

The larger and small circles represent bodies in two different realms, the physical and the spiritual. Ordinarily, these realms are completely independent, but in human personality they are united by the unifying body, which shares something of the nature of both, and so is represented by the middle sized circle.

Figure 1 is our normal body in waking moments.

Figure 2 is our normal body when asleep, unconscious, or in trance. It is also the first stage of the process of death, but as long as the two bodies are connected by the cord there is no decay, and life may be restored. At what stage the quick review of the whole life takes place is not sure. It may be either here or possibly as late as the end of the Hades period.

Figure 3 is the Hades period, the time of adjustment between worlds. The soul is still tied to the vehicle of vitality and hence is dazed if not fully asleep.

In Figure 4 the vehicle of vitality has also been discarded somewhat as a space-ship discards the first stage rocket which has pushed it from earth, and which thereafter would be only a hindrance.

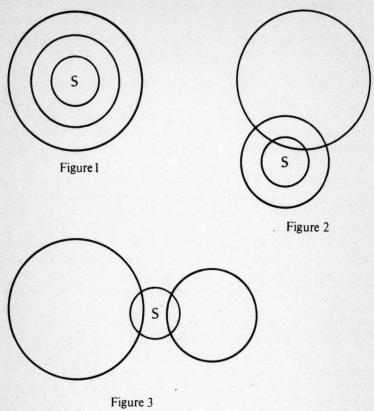

Figure 1

Figure 2

Figure 3

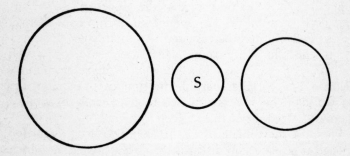

Figure 4

The timing of this process has to be uncertain, but the traditions of most races have come up with a period of from two to four days as the time which should elapse before burial.

Crookall, in checking a large number of reports, discovered a quite different experience when a violent death was caused by an explosion rather than by a blow or asphyxiation. Apparently the spirit body is also damaged and takes some time, often weeks, to recover. During this time there is no conscious awareness. The silver cord is also destroyed.[16]

This is a strange story, far different from the ideas of most of those who have not considered the evidence in the light of the Four Watchmen of science. Yet it seems to be the general picture required by the combination of logic and fact. Actually, there is less difference between this outline of a three-day voyage to paradise and traditional ideas of either science or religion than that between advances which have taken place in the last hundred years as the result of the application of the methods of science to old ideas. Consider, for example, our understanding of astronomy in terms of galaxies, and possibly of curved space, as compared to the ideas of a flat earth. Who could have conceived of atomic power, or television, or voyages to the moon, even half a century ago? Every advance has come as the discovery of new facts or the re-examination of old phenomena, and then through seeking to confirm the conclusions of reason in the laboratory of experience. The picture here given cannot be tested in a physics laboratory or by space travellers. It must remain an adventure of faith which each man makes for himself, and confirms in his own experience.

> To every man there openeth
> A way, and ways, and the Way,
> And the High Soul climbs the High Way,
> And the low soul gropes the low;
> And in between on the misty flats
> The rest drift to and fro.
> But to every man there openeth
> A High Way and a Low,
> And every man decideth
> Which way his soul shall go.
>   *John Oxenham*

8 Heaven at Last?

Heaven at last? But let's call it paradise, as it is not the final heaven, but rather a halfway house on the path from self to God. Yet its life is the life of heaven as most of us picture it. Anything beyond is indescribable, or "unspeakable" as St Paul put it, and is beyond the theme of this book.

The subject of our last chapter was Hades, the Sheol of the ancient Hebrews, and the underworld of the Greeks and Romans. While it is possible to remain in it indefinitely as 'earthbound souls', most of us pass through it quickly, often sleeping the whole time, and so will remember very little about it. It is primarily a transitional stage between earth and paradise, serving the purposes already described and providing a bridge between the two worlds. Now we are through with it, and are ready for whatever God has prepared for us.

Paradise is the earth-like next world of 'many mansions' or realms where we are sure to find a place prepared for us when we are ready for it. It is the waiting world in which we will feel perfectly at home when the time comes. It is the reality which this book has been seeking to demonstrate, and for which, in one sense, our whole previous life on earth has been a preparation. This is not to say that it is the ultimate, or even that there is a *ne plus ultra*, a place beyond which there is nothing. Yet surely there are realms ahead, as far beyond our present grasp as is the soul of a saint beyond a butterfly. Paradise is 'down to earth' both in terms of location and of condition. Yet there are differences, as we shall see.

We wake up in paradise with little or no memory of Hades, and only slowly become aware of who we are and of the earthlife we have left behind. If we are still conscious of earth surroundings we are not in paradise because, with the cutting of the silver cord we can no longer return to the physical body, and with the dropping of the vehicle of vitality we can no longer see or contact earth — except under certain conditions which will be discussed later. As we become acclimatized to this strange new world we discover it is not so different from the existence we have known.

We will be ourselves! Our memories, thoughts, prejudices, habits of thinking and speaking, knowledge and skills, our likes and dislikes will all be unchanged — at least at first. One difference that will appear is that our sharpness of perception and clarity of thinking will be greater than ever before. We will be surprised at how alive and alert we are. Practically all evidence confirms what Swedenborg has written:

"Men think, also, after death, far more perspicuously and distinctly than during their previous life; for in a spiritual state of being more is involved in one idea than in a thousand whilst in the natural life. . . In a word, man loses nothing by death, but is still a man in all respects, although more perfect than when in the body."[1]

Our bodies also will be just as real in paradise as on earth. According to Swedenborg again:

"He is in a body as he was in the natural world; and to all appearances there is no difference. But his body is spiritual, and is therefore separated or purified from all things terrestial. And what is spiritual touches and sees what is spiritual . . . A human spirit also enjoys every sense, external and internal, which he enjoyed in the world. He sees as before, hears and speaks as before, smells and tastes as before, and feels when he is touched. He also longs, desires, craves, thinks, reflects, is stirred, loves, wills, as he did previously."[2]

But this is not the whole story. Physical defects and injuries are not usually carried over into the next life. The spirit body will be found to be perfect in form and function. A physical leg may be amputated or an eye lost, but not in the life beyond. In time it will be realized that the earthly physical body is but an imperfect shadow or creation of the perfect soul body. This is the basis, incidentally, for many spiritual healings of physical diseases and defects. Through faith and prayer sufficient spiritual energy is provided to restore the physical body to the likeness of the undamaged spiritual or soul body.

We will also discover paradise to be a world of beauty beyond anything we have ever conceived possible. Most frequent are reports of a lovely brook, a winding path, and wild flowers often of species and colors unknown to earth. There will be trees and grass, birds and animals, and all will be bathed in unfading light, reminiscent of the vision of John on Patmos: "And night shall be no more; and they need no light of lamp or sun, for the Lord God will be their light." (Revelations 22:5)

There will be differences depending on the desires and dreams of the individual. Flowers will not fade, nor weeds crowd them out. "They shall not hurt or destroy in all my holy mountain" as Isaiah sang (11:9). And there will be dogs and horses for those who love them, lakes and mountains, and even great cities.

One of the obvious problems we have in trying to outline the life beyond is a result of our concept of time and timing. There are no clocks based on the movements of the physical earth. Time seems to be not merely a psychological experience in paradise, but a reality beyond anything we can grasp in our physical bodies. Stewart Edward White calls it 'orthic time' in his *Unobstructed Universe*, but our most familiar reference to it is in Psalm 90: "For a thousand years in thy sight are but as yesterday when it is past, or as a watch in the night." When we add to this the wide variety of experiences in Hades which depend on the multitudinous varieties of consciousness in individuals, as well as the varied circumstances under which death takes place, it becomes clearly impossible to be very definite.

This is obvious in the matter of a reception committee of friends or being found by spirit guides. Deathbed experiences indicate that many people are met immediately, but never when they have had no belief in another life. There also seem to be stubborn souls who refuse to believe, and others of such perverted desires that their eyes are closed, and who are earthbound until they are ready to change. Further confusion grows out of the fact that many sleep through the Hades experience, so have no recollection of it at all.

The one certainty in all of this is that we are loved, and that the reality is better than any teachings we have received or any pictures we can ourselves conceive. All reports agree that we are met and introduced into a new life, usually by old friends and relatives who have preceded us in death — or better, *into life,* as there is no such thing as death. Recognition will partly be by familiar clothing and mannerisms, but more by an inner knowing. They will make us feel at home — indeed, if we die in old age or after a long sickness, we may find a home prepared for us with many of our dearest friends in similar surroundings around us.

There are some things we will not need. Money is useless. Nothing can be purchased because everything we need is provided as we learn to think and ask. The promise of Jesus is literally true, "Ask, and you will receive." There are banquets for those who want them, or we may simply gain strength and nourishment from the air, just as the soul does during sleep in this life. Clothing is provided by thought in such amounts and forms as we deem fitting. There is a house for us, alone or with others, or we can design and create our own with lawns and gardens that never require cutting or watering. Paradise is indeed the land of heart's desire!

Likewise there are some things in this present physical life that we may want to escape. There is no physical pain or weakness, no work that must be done, jails, dirty jobs, or alarm clocks. There are no accidents by which we may break our legs, or lose our lives. In paradise we are sentenced, not to death, but to life, and there is no escape even by suicide. We cannot run away — particularly from ourselves. The threat of scripture that even our secret thoughts will all be known becomes a terrible reality. There is no hiding or putting up a front. Our emotions of any and every kind will be visible for all to see. "There is no hiding place there."

As we go farther and learn to use our new gifts and powers we learn that we can travel by thought. We have but to think of a place, and lo, we are there! We picture a friend, and we are together — providing it is mutually desired. We learn to communicate by thought much more rapidly than by words.

No wonder that the glories of paradise are 'unspeakable'. Both communication and creation depend on the disciplined powers of the mind to focus attention and desire in detail. What a life!

Like every earthly capacity the privileges of paradise must be learned and directed if they are to be fruitful. They may be misused or wasted just as long as we desire. Note how Myers confirms this:

"Nearly every soul lives for a time in the state of illusion . . . On earth he longed for a superior brand of cigar. He can have the experience *ad nauseam* of smoking this brand. He wanted to play golf, so he plays golf. But he is merely dreaming all the time, or rather, living within the fantasy created by his strongest desires on earth. After a while this life of pleasure ceases to amuse and content him. Then he begins to think and long for the unknown, to long for a new life. He is at last prepared to make the leap in evolution and this cloudy dream vanishes."[3]

We are now ready for helpful work and further education, and to join in the myriad of activities available in paradise. There are unlimited opportunities for study and growth in great libraries and lecture halls, for music and art and worship. Much scientific progress on earth is preceded by similar discoveries in the next world. There are no limits except our willingness to grow by persistent application.

Assignments of even more satisfying work to do or services to be rendered are made or chosen on the basis of our interests and needs. Some are trained to meet new arrivals who are the victims of accident or war, whose friends and relatives have therefore not been alerted to their coming. Many of them become guardian angels for their charges. This is an ancient tradition which has become real to me as a result of personal experiences with two non-professional mediums. Each reported the same type of personality and description, and then spoke in what seemed to me to be the same voice. It may be that I am gullible or superstitious, but as my personal awareness has increased in recent years it has often seemed to me that I was guided or guarded, and sometimes warned — but never saved from the results of my own stubborn folly. Swedenborg puts it this way:

"Angels of every society are sent to men, that they may guard them, and withdraw them from evil affections, and consequent evil thoughts, and inspire them with good affections, so far as they are willing to receive them from freedom."[4]

One interesting story which has come to me is about Don, the son of the writers Laurence and Frances Dunlop Heron. He died while in his junior year at Princeton, specializing in international relations. The parents were conventional Christians who did not believe in communication with the dead, and who accepted its reality only after a series of sittings with mediums on both sides of the Atlantic. During these Don came through again and again with the zest and vitality of a college boy writing to his parents. His assignment was working for peace with some of the delegates to the United Nations. He reported greater success with the representatives of the smaller and newer countries of Africa than with those of the older and stronger nations. The whole story was written up and syndicated in a number of the leading church publications of the United States and Canada under the title 'The Psychic Challenge to the Churches'.

The occupations of paradise run the whole gamut of human interests except making money, crime and punishment, rendering physical services, or providing food, clothing or other goods. There are colleges and schools of all kinds, music halls, places of worship, most of which are in the open. Here is an excerpt from an article from the ouija board of Robert and Anita Smith of South Natick, Massachusetts:[5]

"Here [in paradise] we do have many who find in teaching a course in helping themselves whilst helping others. There are those who comfort; those who work side by side with your scientists, your social workers, ministers, doctors, artists of all kinds; in fact most every endeavor which helps mankind."

The medical schools mentioned in the story of Dr Philip (in Chapter V) most certainly had to do with the healing of physical bodies, presumably of persons on earth. There is considerable evidence that spirit doctors work constantly with those on this side of death.

Sickness in paradise is primarily the result of negative emotions. Let Raynor Johnson, atomic physicist and one of the most careful and scientific writers in this field describe it:

"Diseases of the astral (soul) body are not merely unpleasant to perceive, they also create a radiation of an unpleasant and even painful kind to which those around them are subjected. Treatment is therefore essential if the society of such persons is to be acceptable to others. The physician's work of the astral level (paradise) calls for great devotion and self-sacrifice, for he must subject himself to the unpleasant symptoms from which his patients are suffering. Where treatment is ineffective and cure is not possible, such persons prefer to seek a lower level where their condition is more easily tolerated. The positive emotions of love, kindness, goodwill, and compassion are said to be beautiful and radiant in the astral (soul) body, and properly directed and used can be powerful instruments of healing."[6]

This brings us to appearance in paradise. Except in the lower regions just mentioned, it seems that we look as we feel we should at the time of life we consider most nearly perfect. This means that the old are younger, and the young generally older. It will be recalled that Dr Wiltse (Chapter IV) was pleasantly surprised to find that he was considerably larger in his soul body, though when he later returned to his earth body he had not changed at all. When greeting newcomers from earth for the first time we are able to assume the appearance and clothing, even to becoming little children, by which we will be easily recognized.

As for children in paradise, let me quote Swedenborg again. Although he lived in an age when unbaptized infants were thought to be damned to burn in hell forever, he wrote: "Every little child, wheresoever born, . . . is received by the Lord at death; is educated in heaven (paradise) . . . and becomes an angel."[7] He goes on to say that children are also specially educated for marriage in paradise if they so desire, and that they find their partners supposedly by chance, and recognize them immediately.

If this is true, then not only are some earthly marriages made in heaven, but there are also heavenly ones. This raises the whole question of sex and marriage in the future life. It is usually assumed that the statement of Jesus in Luke 20:34-36 disposed of the matter:

"The sons of this age marry and are given in marriage; but those who are accounted worthy to attain to that age and to the resurrection from the dead neither marry nor are given in marriage, for they cannot die any more, because they are equal to the angels and are sons of God."

But not so is the almost unanimous testimony from the other side. Those who mention this statement of Jesus seem to agree that it belongs only to the higher regions beyond even the third heaven of St Paul. Of course there is no childbirth beyond this life, and it may well be that the relationships in paradise have nothing to do with physical sex. Here let me quote again, firstly from the oldest of the books in front of me, written by Swedenborg, an old bachelor living in a time of great moral laxity who might well be expected to be as opposed to marriage as was St Paul:

"Now since conjugal love is the most fundamental love of all good loves, . . . it follows that the delights of that love exceed the delights of all other loves . . . The reason why all delights are collected in this love, is on account of the surpassing excellence of its use: its use is the propagation of the human race, and hence of the angelic heaven, and as this use was the end of ends of creation that all the blessedness, blissfulness, delights, joys and pleasures which could be possibly conferred upon man by the Lord the Creator, are collected into this his love.

"Married partners, who have lived a truly conjugal love, are not separated in the death of one of them. For the spirit of the deceased partner lives continually with the spirit of the other, not yet deceased, and this even to the death of the other, when they meet again and reunite, and love each other more tenderly than before; for now they are in the spiritual world."[8]

"They [the angels] declare . . . there are few who are in genuine marriage . . . while the delight of true marriage not only endures to old age in the world, but after death becomes the delight of heaven, and is there filled with an interior delight that grows more and more perfect in eternity."[9]

In Bishop James A. Pike's book, *The Other Side*, there is an account of a seance of the Bishop with a Mrs Ena Twigg in London, when he was having a conversation with his son,

Jim, who had recently committed suicide. Jim has just expressed his desire to know more people, and to know them better.

" 'Do you think of people there as male and female?' I continued. 'Is there anything like — like intimate expression?'

"The terms of the answer seemed almost to express amusement at my delicacy of expression; it was very much like Jim. Without a pause: 'Sex? Yes, there is sex, but it is not like it is there. It is not physical, of course, but actually there is less limitation. It is more obviously what sex really means. Here you can actually enter the whole person. It is like you are in fact merging — becoming one.' "[10]

Many other illustrations could be given, but they would all amount to the same thing. After examining hundreds of reports of the life beyond in relation to sex, R. DeWitt Miller summarizes them as follows:

"Sexual pleasures 'over there' are chosen, as they are to a limited extent here, by the individual, and that choice is the result of spiritual, intellectual, ethical, and artistic development . . . Also communications invariably indicate that sexual ecstasy in this life is only a foretaste of something more exquisite in the next. The full potentialities of sex are but glimpsed here. They are the shape of things to come."[11]

Fellowship and friendship are among the greatest joys of paradise. We are not restricted to those we have already known, but there are great societies of congenial souls, and the opportunities for new and greater friendships simply for their own sake, or as a companionship in service, are without limit. Perhaps a picture of part of another session with Arthur Ford in 1958 may illustrate. Present also were half a dozen minister friends, some of them very sceptical about the whole matter. I do not have a tape record, but the gist of it is very clear in my mind.

One of those who came through from the other side was a missionary doctor who had been befriended by my friend, Ned, at the time of his last illness and death, and he wanted to express his appreciation. Ned confirmed it in some detail. Another who came introduced himself as the father of Jerry, another minister present. The interesting thing was that the father had become acquainted with the missionary while in paradise though they had never met previously, and that he, the father, had got the missionary doctor to work with his son, Jerry, in the development of healing through prayer — a field that was of increasing interest to Jerry, and which he later promoted in his denomination.

This seems a simple thing, but notice some of the implications: two men who have been complete strangers become friends in the next life. One persuades his new friend to help his son in a phase of spiritual growth. Both have work to do and are in touch with friends still in the body, helping wherever they can. The Ford seance, to which both Ned and Jerry were invited, gave them an opportunity to reveal themselves and what they were doing, and so give evidence of a continued life of love and activity in the next world. No one person knew all the facts that were brought out, but together they were able to confirm them. I might add that Ford knew neither of the ministers, nor that they were to be present that night.

Paradise is apparently so much like our present world that we will feel perfectly at home in it. While its areas are without limit, as far as we can see we are assigned or find our way to a community of like-minded souls, many of them relatives and old friends. Although there are no telephones it seems that we can contact each other at will when it is mutually desired. However, we can also leave the hook off the receiver, so to speak, and not be bothered by intruders or salesmen! One opportunity for growth that is missing, on the other hand, is the challenge of getting along with disagreeable persons or financial problems, or even with difficult children and irritating husbands and wives. It makes for easy living, but not for spiritual growth, even if there are lessons to learn and work to do. We can take a thousand years if we so desire as there are no jangling alarm clocks to get us up or monthly bills to pay.

The various parts of paradise can perhaps be illustrated by an account of communications between members of a family, some in paradise and others still on earth, as quoted by Raynor Johnson:

"There are great cities over here for people who like cities. Harold has taken me on a short visit to purgatory which is another London . . . But this etheric London isn't all purgatory. There are some lovely people living contentedly in small houses on rather grubby streets. They were good souls, but such streets were their idea of heaven, so they found it. They will gradually be weaned away from this shabby idea of paradise when they learn to throw themselves more outward, when they use the wings of their minds and visit other peoples' worlds."[12]

One question we are bound to ask about the many communications, so-called, from which I have quoted is: how can paradise be a paradise if there is an awareness of all that is happening on earth, the suffering and cruelty, the poverty and hatreds? There are several answers. One is that we are only aware as we want to be, as we really care. Of course one price of love is suffering. This is as true for man as for God, and paradise would be hell indeed if it were gained only by losing love.

Another possible answer may be deduced from a personal experience during World War II. We had just learned of the death of a close friend on Iwo Jima, and the futility and tragedy of war stood out in dark outline in the wasting of this choice young life, the only son of a widowed mother. I was coming downstairs when it seemed that I suddenly knew reality — reality with an utter certainty beyond all human reason. It was not an argument, nor a vision, nor a voice, but a certainty beyond my power to doubt. I sensed Bert's death as God must see it in terms of a strange comparison. When our own son was about three, he tripped and fell on the pavement, and came in crying and with a very bloody nose. I wiped away the blood and tried to comfort him, all the time knowing that there would be many tears and nosebleeds in the years ahead, but they would all be forgotten in the strength of manhood.

So I knew the Heavenly Father was comforting us in our sorrow, yet sensing also that it would be nothing more than a nosebleed in the long vista of life ahead. After more than twenty years the assurance and comfort of this experience is as vivid and real to me as it was at the time. Could it be that this was a preview of one aspect of the consciousness of paradise, a sure knowledge that the sins and sufferings of these tragic days will be swallowed up in the joy when men and nations grow up into what Jesus called the Kingdom of Heaven?

We have spoken about the knowledge of earth open to those in paradise. How about the kind of communication involved in seances and automatic writing? Many hints are given that this is often difficult and sometimes painful, requiring the lowering of one's vibrations to something comparable to the level of Hades in order to communicate with those who have mediumistic powers in one way or another. This usually seems to result in a lower level of consciousness corresponding to that of the shadowy dream world of Hades, and often lower than that of earth. This is one explanation of the seeming banality of many communications, and the frequent forgetfulness of names and incidents.

In the report of two contacts with Roy Burkhart (in Chapter VI), I mentioned that something was missing. He was in character all right, but dull and prosaic compared with the sparkle and humor and quick repartee we had known in Roy. If this was Roy Burkhart, and I feel it was, he had greatly deteriorated. If this was paradise, I would want nothing of it. However, I have now come to realize that this was the temporary price he had to pay in order to continue some of the plans cut off by his sudden transition. For my first transcontinental phone call about fifty years ago I had to go to a dirty phone booth and pay five dollars for a very poor connection with the girl who is now my wife. Even that was worthwhile — and I am sure Roy Burkhart felt it was worth it too, under the conditions.

Frederic Myers, communicating through Geraldine Cummins, has an explanation of this:

"Your soul is only aware of those beings who possess bodies vibrating with the same intensity . . . he may go back, temporarily descend a rung of the ladder and make mental contact with a soul who inhabits a denser shape. He can even descend into Hades, enter its fog and come into contact with human beings . . . and it is as if the memory of his experiences on a higher plane were temporarily anaesthetized away. So he is incapable of conveying to earth, save with rare exceptions, any interesting or remarkable information. Caught in the cocoon of earth memories . . . he can merely speak of trivial material affairs.''[13]

In any case all agree that the joy and humor of paradise are beyond anything we know on earth. We have a few glimpses of it in the New Testament, but as far as I am concerned it is primarily a matter of faith. We see through a glass darkly only a shadow of the glory beyond. Most human speech is incidental and inconsequential, and we should expect nothing more from our beloved when they have moved on. They take with them only what they are, and when they talk back they cannot even reveal the best of their earthly lives, partly because their minds are dulled and ours confused.

One final question is certain to come up. If paradise is so wonderful, even with the limitations we have mentioned, why would anybody want to get out of it? Most of us are aware that even the best of situations become boring. There is something in the human spirit, whether on earth or in heaven, which is never quite satisfied for very long. Even with all the variety of friendships, of things to learn and do, and of ideas and places to explore in a realm far greater than this earth, its challenge ultimately runs out. Sooner or later we learn why Myers calls it 'the plane of illusion', and we want to leave. This may be after what in earth time would be fifty, or even a thousand, years. According to Catholic doctrine some saints may skip paradise and move on to the true heaven just as the average person skips Hades in several days. Gloria Lee, whose *The Going and the Glory* has been quoted, was in the heavenly realm in a matter of months, while Frederic Myers took several years, but these were both advanced souls. As long as we enjoy paradise we stay there.

What then? This is beyond the purview and hypothesis of this book. Several possibilities can be mentioned for those who want to consider them. We may move on into the third heaven if we are ready for it. This means shedding the soul body — another death and birth. Little is told us about this, though we still have bodies and are said to be spatially related to earth. The realms beyond this — well, they are beyond.

There is another possibility because, as the Negro spiritual puts it, "Everybody talkin' about heaven, ain't goin' there." This brings up the question of reincarnation, or even of life on other planets, which, again, is not our subject. Yet most communicators seem to agree on one or both of these, more or less, although a few are violently opposed — another illustration that the prejudices of earth are carried over into the realms beyond. Logic seems to say that if we do not learn the lessons of earth this time we may have to repeat a class, here or elsewhere. Or it may be that there are other lessons waiting which can better be taught in the rough and tumble of earth than in the summerland of paradise.

The idea of life on other planets has always fascinated mankind — at least since the time of Galileo and the discovery that they were similar to our earth in some ways. Even Myers, through the hand of Geraldine Cummins, writes: [14]

"Human beings exist on certain planets, but their bodies are subject to a different time from earth time, and travel, therefore, within the rhythm of different time from that time. Consequently their physical parts are either vibrating slower or faster than yours, and may not be discovered through the medium of man's senses."

Swedenborg also claims that other planets and moons are inhabited and gives a similar explanation why our human senses will never be able to detect them. Our space travellers will find apparently dead and empty planets just as science fiction time travellers from the past could know nothing of the wonders and beauties of television without the instruments for tuning in.

But life is larger than logic and fact is truer than fancy. I do not know. It has been only a few years since most of the material in this book would have been considered illogical, heretical and incomprehensible fantasy to me — even if it had been called to my attention. Perhaps we should all be more humble and join with Oliver Wendell Holmes in his aspiration:

Build thee more stately mansions, O my soul
   As the swift seasons roll!
   Leave thy low-vaulted past!
Let each new temple, nobler than the last,
Shut thee from heaven with a dome more vast,
    Till thou at length art free,
Leaving thine outgrown shell by life's unresting sea.

9 Yes, there is Hell

We have talked about Hades, paradise and heaven: how about hell? The word is certainly a part of our common vocabulary and possibly of everyday thought, but is it a fact of life or merely a figure of speech? Are we sent there, or do we take it with us wherever we may go at death? Was Milton right: "Myself am hell?"

These and many similar questions have been skirted along the way in several previous chapters. It may be said that science has no answers, while theology has all too many. It was clear in our brief study of the Old Testament that no consistent concept of either heaven or hell was to be found. The clearest picture was of Sheol, the Hebrew word for Hades, as the destination of all the dead regardless of moral worth or spiritual development in this life. It is described as a shadowy underworld separated from man and God in Psalm 88 (quoted in Chapter XI).

The New Testament is equally inconsistent; nor is it clear when phrases like 'hellfire' and 'lake of fire and brimstone' are to be taken literally or figuratively. The word translated as 'hell' in the revised versions is *ghenna,* the city dump in the gulch of Hinnom outside of Jerusalem where trash was always burning. Not too much can be made of that.

However, when we examine the teachings and practice of Jesus in the light of the paranormal, especially astral projection and mediumship, we find many reasons for believing in a very real hell, although somewhat different from that of traditional belief.

Let us first take a look at so-called demon possession. There is no doubt about the teaching and example of Jesus on this point. The disciples were amazed that they also could cast out demons (Luke 10:17-20), although they did not always succeed (Mark 9:14-18). The practice declined in the early church although it has reappeared from time to time throughout Christian history. The modern world, and along with it much of the present-day church, has tended to consider it either a superstition of primative peoples or as something that ended with the New Testament.

However, the idea of a spiritual world of evil as well as of good, a world populated by 'the devil and his angels' (Matthew 25:41), including those who once served him in physical bodies, and who seek to seduce or possess men on earth, opens up the idea of a very real hell as the next dwelling place of many souls on earth. Before we drop this as superstition, let me summarize four stories, all of them from unimpeachable sources.

The first was told me by a cousin of mine, a prominent Presbyterian missionary in Korea shortly after the turn of the century. He was trying to tell the story of Jesus in a little village where it had never been heard, but was constantly interrupted by a woman who was apparently insane. Finally, under a great sense of urgency, he commanded, in the name of Jesus Christ, the demon to leave her. The woman went into convulsions and in a few minutes came out of them completely sane. There was no more trouble.

The second is about a Christian Science woman practitioner who was asked by a medical doctor to help with a woman who was murderously insane. Being left alone with the practitioner the patient tried to choke her to death, but was stopped by the patient's daughter. When the practitioner recovered her breath she shouted, "You devil, you get out of that woman and never bother her again." The woman quieted down and was soon stroking the hand of the practitioner, completely harmless. The trouble did not return.

The third was about a psychiatrist who told a friend of mine, the pastor of a large Congregational church in the Middle West, about his strange discovery. He was having almost miraculous success with many of his mental patients after he learned that he could command the evil spirits to leave in the name of Christ, just as was done in the early church and by my cousin in Korea. However, he did not dare tell his professional colleagues for fear they would think he needed treatment himself; but he simply had to tell someone, so he went to his pastor, who told me.

I will tell the fourth in more detail not only because I know all the persons involved, but because of its importance to our subject. A very fine young woman whom my wife and I have known for many years became in the course of a few weeks a chain smoker, an alcoholic with weekly binges, and a morphine addict. Finally friends in desperation went to a minister whose wife is a medium, to see if they could find any explanation. I have in my files the stenographic transcription of the tape of the seance which lasted about an hour, but I will only summarize it here.

The tape consists of a dialogue between the minister and a crude, pugnacious voice which broke in without invitation, speaking through the medium who was in semi-trance. The voice claimed that he was the father of the girl, that she had belonged to him as a wife or mistress in two previous life-times, that she was supposed to have been his wife in this life, but came as his daughter instead. He admitted having betrayed her sexually as a girl, and was still determined to have her at any cost. Because she had previously given herself to him he was able to possess her, and was using nicotine, alcohol and morphine as progressive steps by which to destroy her body so she could be with him as his wife in the spirit world.

After a long argument the minister finally said that in the name of Jesus Christ he was drawing a ring of fire about the father so he could not escape until he wanted to repair the damage he had done. When the spirit realized he was actually trapped, he said he would give the girl up, but the minister insisted that he was an eternal soul who needed help, and would receive it whenever he honestly wanted it. The seance ended on this note.

The pay off was interesting. That same evening the girl, knowing nothing of the seance, was pacing back and forth like a wild creature in the home of a mutual friend. Suddenly, and as far as could be determined, at just the time the spirit of her father said he would give her up, she sat down quietly and was her old self for the first time in a month. It took her some two weeks to get over smoking, drinking and drug-taking, without any special help. She is still her fine old self knowing nothing, as I understand it, except that those months were a nightmare. The whole experience, in part of which I was personally involved, convinced me more than any thing else of the reality of hell.

Another type of experience involves an entirely different kind of ghost from those described in Chapter IV who usually come at the time of death or shortly thereafter to say that they are still alive and to bring comfort to their families or friends; and sometimes to complete something they had failed to do while still alive in their physical bodies.

This last type, on the other hand, is often involved with haunted houses, poltergeist phenomena, as well as some fairly rare types of experiences commonly supposed to be nothing more than superstition. The subject is complicated and all of my knowledge of it is second-hand, so I am not going to discuss it except to point out its relation to our theme at this point. If there is any reality to it, and the evidence of much investigation points in that direction, it fits in with the idea that there are great numbers in the spirit world who have not got further than the conditions of Hades, either because of the evil they have chosen, or because of an undeveloped spiritual and intellectual life.

I have a friend, a minister's wife and a high school teacher, a woman of great spiritual and mental discrimination, who is aware of a spirit world all about us. She and her husband had to move from one lovely home they owned because she could not go out in the front garden without being aware of a spirit chained to a tree. She was able to communicate with him and learned that he had committed murder, and could not leave the place until the time his victim normally would have died. I never knew who sentenced him to this, or whether he had accepted it for himself as one way he could make expiation.

All of this is certainly far different from my childhood picture and the hellfire and brimstone sometimes still preached. As for location, it is apparently all about us, as are also both paradise and heaven. It is primarily a state of consciousness, not a place. The geography of the life beyond is one thing not clearly taught in books, but it is more a matter of semantics than of practice. Swedenborg makes it a separate area where the evil choose to go because only there do they find themselves at home. He is very definite in *Arcana Coelestia*:[1] "The Lord never sends anyone into hell, but is desirous to bring all out; ... but since the evil spirit rushes into it himself, the Lord turns all punishment to some good and use."

All reports agree that we have to face the possibility of hell not because God wants to get even, or that we must suffer so much pain in order to balance so much evil, *quid pro quo,* an eye for an eye. Nor did Jesus die to appease an angry God or to buy us back from the devil, but in order to reveal the love and forgiveness of a loving Father, and to empty hell. Nobody finds himself in hell for what he believed or did not believe, for being a pagan or agnostic, a savage or even a member of a certain church. Some modern Roman Catholic theologians get around the problem by insisting that there has to be the traditional hell, but that nowhere is it claimed that it has to be inhabited.

It is interesting to note the similarity, in spite of differences of style and philosophy, of the reports of Swedenborg two and a half centuries ago of astral travel, and that of Myers fifty years ago writing through the hand of a gifted medium. So Swedenborg wrote in *Heaven and Hell:*

"From every hell there exhales a sphere of the lusts in which the inhabitants are. When this sphere is perceived by one who is in similar lust, he is affected in heart, and is filled with delight; for lust and its delight make one, since whatever any one lusts after is delightful toward him. Hence the spirit turns himself toward the hell whence the sphere proceeds, and from delight of heart longs to go thither, for as yet he is not aware that such torments exist there; and he who knows it, still desires to go there; for no one in the spiritual world can resist his own lust ..."[2]

After referring to a passage on the final page of the New Testament "Let the evil doer still do evil, and the filthy still be filthy," (Revelations 22:11) Myers goes on to comment:

"The man that comes into this life with a sex history of a

reprehensible kind finds, when he enters the Kingdom of the Mind, that as his mental perceptions are sharpened so his predominant earth desire is intensified, his mental power being far more considerable. He can at will summon to himself those who will gratify this overdeveloped side of his nature. Others of his kind will gravitate to him. And for a time these beings live in a sex paradise . . . They obtain it in abundance and there follows a terrible satiety. They come to loathe what they can obtain with ease . . ."[3]

Could it be that this is the reality behind the traditional idea of purgatory? Could this be the flame in the parable of the rich man and Lazarus (Luke 16:19-31)? Whether the rich man was in hell or Hades, or even a lower part of paradise — a sex paradise as suggested by Myers — really makes no difference. The reality was there. The flames may be a burning sense of shame, or the burning of self-will as was suggested by some of the medieval mystics, but they are no less painful.

From all of this it is clear that hell is a temporary state, lasting until we have had enough and are ready to change. It is likely, as some communicators claim, that we are earthbound either because of our love of earth, or, that because of ignorance, stubbornness or pride, we refuse to move on into paradise, but cling to earth as long as we can. This apparently was so with the father who sought to possess his daughter and bring her to himself for sexual enjoyment.

This also fits in with our second scientific assumption that there is no growth or change without an adequate cause or combination of causes to account for it. Therefore we are exactly the person just after death that we were just before death. The things we chose to do and be, we still desire and are. We continue in the same direction until we choose to exercise our freedom to change, and this may be no easier than breaking an ingrained habit in this life. Newton's law of inertia is as true in the spiritual realm as in the physical.

Somewhere along the line in paradise comes the judgement. The time seems to depend on spiritual readiness. With highly developed souls it may be very early, or it may be centuries later in terms of earth time before we are able to face our spiritual immaturity and see ourselves as we really are in relation to what we should be and can become.

It is not a universal judgement before the King or a panel of judges at the end of the world or at the return of Christ to earth, but a very personal individual experience during which we again see the scroll of our past life in reverse, as we often quickly do during the process of violent death. This time, however, it is a slow and careful review of our past during which we enter into the full emotional experiences of those we have both hurt and helped. We are both judge and jury as, with sharpened sensibilities, we see and feel the full impact of our life for both good and evil. It can be a terrible experience — hell indeed!

Lest this chapter be too painful, let me quote from a lighter description. *The Going and the Glory* purports to be by Gloria Lee, an attractive and vivacious young California woman who died as a result of a protracted fast in 1962. Shortly after this a medium in Miami, Florida, claimed that she had received word from Gloria that she would be communicating through a medium in New Zealand who had no knowledge of her in the physical body, and so would not be prejudiced one way or another. A few weeks later in Auckland, New Zealand, 'Verity' began to hear from a spirit who identified herself as Gloria Lee through automatic writing. In ten days some 35,000 words were transmitted. Although some of it goes beyond the scope of this book, most of it is entirely consistent with all I have come to understand and accept about the waiting world. I quote.

"The glory was not yet because I first had to judge myself . . . It was then that I became aware of Cosmic Memory . . . which registers with unfailing accuracy the thoughts and actions of every living soul . . . At a given moment after the entity leaves earth, making the transition called death, the Cosmic Computer goes into action. It operates projector fashion, and is vividly clear and more beautifully colored than any mortal film . . .

"In my moment of truth it began to pay back my life on earth, *but in reverse.* Therefore the first thing I saw quite clearly was my lifeless form surrounded by the grief auras of others. The tape stopped momentarily because I, too, had to share in the emotions I had so thoughtlessly thrust upon others. And that is the answer to the Day of Judgment. No

Karmic Board, no Hierarchal Board, sits or stands sentinel. We are very much alone in the moment of Truth. In what seemed to me to be a great lonely vault of a place I was watching a character called Gloria Lee going about her daily life on the earth plane. All the mannerisms I'd affected, the irritating habits I'd formed, were run off for me to see. But, from the new level, we are given a spiritual gift of judging what we see objectively — and such objectivity is razor sharp. Its immediate effect made me want to pare away the bruised parts of me that did not measure up to the Christ consciousness. To say it was an uncomfortable experience is to put it mildly. It can be downright agonizing to view yourself as others see you."[4]

What follows this is sometimes called the assignment, but it is self-chosen. If we are in hell it is because that is our choice. It is the only place where we are happy, or even comfortable. The paradise described in the previous chapter is open to us, except that the New Testament threat that every secret thought shall be known (Mark 4:22, Luke 12:2, 3, etc.) is absolutely true. In the earth life both clothing and the physical body serve to hide and often disguise what we really are and think, but in the next life all evidence agrees that we are seen and known exactly as we are. "There is no hiding place there."

It is said that in a nudist colony the person wearing clothing will feel so uncomfortable that he is soon forced either to disrobe or to leave. In the life beyond we are all so completely naked in the spiritual sense that we can never rest satisfied until we find the company of those of like mind. Swedenborg deals with this in tiresome detail. Myers expresses the same idea through Geraldine Cummins in *The Road to Immortality:*[5] "If you are what I term Animal-man . . . you will desire to go downward, that is to say, you will choose to be an inhabitant of matter as dense as the physical body you discarded when you passed into Hades." Hints are given in many places that the reality may be as painful as the symbolism of Dante and Milton. "The history of the cruel man in the hereafter is a book I am not permitted to write," explains Myers in *Beyond Human Personality.*[6]

There is another difference between traditional ideas of

hell and the reality: we may choose to go there, but we do not have to stay, as was previously suggested. Just as soon as we want to change sufficiently to do something about it, we may begin to move up. It cannot be emphasized too much that the door to heaven is always open, and that many spirits from higher realms have accepted the responsibility of going to the assistance of any who call for help. Even the Elder John in Revelation prefaces his terrible imagery of heaven and hell with the promise: (3:8) "Behold, I have set before you an open door, which no one is able to shut."

One group which orthodoxy has always condemned to hellfire are the suicides. Most of the accounts through mediums agree that a person who takes his own life has a hard time of it because he is still himself, very much alive, and still has to face the problems he was seeking to escape. Sometimes it is claimed that he is earthbound until he would normally have died. I do not know. He may have accepted that for himself. Young Jim Pike may have chosen to stay on the Hades level in order to communicate with his father, and help him.

Although we may be sure of general principles, from all the evidence now available this is surely one field where we had better be ignorant about details. Certainly the motive, as of one who wants to free a wife or husband, or of social custom as in medieval Japan or decadent Greece and Rome, would make a difference. In all of this it would be better to "Judge not, that you be not judged," or as probably better translated, "Condemn not, that you be not condemned."

Whenever we go far in examining the stories of those who claim to report back from the life beyond, we find hints that there are many who illustrate what Jesus spoke about in Matthew 12:43: "When the unclean spirit has gone out of a man, he passes through waterless places seeking rest, but who finds none," and who seeks to return to an earth body, "prowling around like a roaring lion, seeking someone to devour". (1 Peter 5:8) Here we have explanations of demon possession in New Testament days and of much insanity and many inexplicable crimes today. This may be an interesting field for speculation, but a dangerous one for personal exploration. We can find hell enough without trying.

Part two

SCIENTIFIC AND DOCTRINAL OBJECTIONS

10 Science—Revelation and Revolution

What a debt we owe to science! It has transformed the world within the memory of many now living. Its physical gifts and gadgets flow forth in an ever-growing torrent. There seems to be nothing it cannot provide except peace, happiness and self-control. What the mind of man can conceive the science of today can provide — anything except the things that matter most. First steam took the burdens off our backs, then electricity put wings on our feet, and now computers do the work of our brains, while the atom makes obsolete all the past forms of power. Only babies have reached for the moon in the past, but now science has made it a reality. What its gifts will be in another century not even science fiction can portray.

So it has become our great god for the same reasons that the sun and the earth were worshipped by primitive man. For out of it have come the treasures we have most prized. By its gifts we seem to live and move and have our being. Or even, as George Bernard Shaw is often quoted as saying, "Science has become the great superstition of the twentieth century." Superstitions always gather around great men — Jesus, Abraham, even Abraham Lincoln — and great movements in history, the founding of nations, the rise of religions. Nor can it be expected that science, the great power above all nations, the new god who seems to answer every prayer and in whose hands are the powers to destroy the race or to bring in a new world, should escape this fate from the hands of its followers. So, before the insights and methodology of science can be turned to the service of the spiritual world its superstitions must be laid bare and its irrational dogmas made clear.

One of the more obvious of these, in the words of Sir Alister Hardy,[1] is "that which is truly scientific will ultimately be explained in terms of physics and chemistry." Related to it is another, quoting from the same source: "Modern evolutionary theory shows that the whole process is an entirely materialistic one leaving no room for the possibility of a spiritual side to man." If these statements are indeed true then the scientist, along with all the rest of us, is "of all men most miserable", for death is the end, and the quicker we come to it the better.

But are they true? Could they not be the illogical and mistaken assumptions of minds untrained in imaginative thinking even though highly skilled in manipulating the tools of physical research? Obsessed by progress in gadgetry and technology, we can no longer hear the whisper of the soul, the still small voice within. The siren voices of radio and television advertising are so pervasive and persuasive, urging us to paint and pamper our bodies as the way to personal and sexual fulfilment, that the ancient word, "Man shall not live by bread alone" can no longer be heard. Therefore it has been easy to assume that anything that cannot be weighed, measured, dissected, or counted must therefore be unreal, a delusion of the imagination not to be considered by practical men. Only that counts which can be counted; only matter matters.

That this is not only a false premise, but a tragic mistake, is indicated by the failure of modern society to hold together. Without any understanding of the nature and destiny of man and with a sense of physical values only, it is small wonder that the greatest age of scientific progress has also seen the most destructive wars and the greatest starvation of all time, not to mention the breakdown of law and order.

But not only is the materialistic premise false and dangerous, it is also comparatively new. As Langdon-Davies put it in *Man and His Universe*,[2] "The whole history of science has been a direct search for God, deliberate and conscious, until well into the eighteenth century. Copernicus, Kepler, Galileo, Newton, Leibnitz and the rest did not merely believe in God in an orthodox sort of way; they believed that their work told humanity more about God than had been known before." Even today, many of the great scientists, especially the physicists, are far from materialists.

Another common misunderstanding of science grows out of the mistaken assumption that the description of a process is an explanation of its origin. For example, to assume that a statement of the theory of evolution thereby explains the presence of man on earth is a fallacy. It is like explaining a watch by naming the sources of its raw materials and describing the processes by which they are formed into a complex mechanism. Equally important, perhaps more so, are the skill and purpose of the watchmaker. There may be substitutes for the raw materials, and it is very possible that different processes of manufacture may be used, but there will never be a watch without a watchmaker, nor a human race without a Creator. This is obvious to common sense, but often forgotten by modern science.

Before we can understand the positive contributions of science to our study of life beyond the body it is necessary to note briefly just what it is and the assumptions which underlie it. Science is first of all a philosophy, a way of thinking about the world and the phenomena of nature, and then of studying and classifying them to discover their uniformities and laws. This is followed by research and invention, creating forms all the way from steam engines to guided missiles and computers. More often science is thought of as a process of deductive and inductive thinking combined with the body of knowledge which has grown out of it. Its methods and results are so familiar that they need not be dwelt upon.

However, it is based on certain unproven, and probably unprovable, assumptions which I have called the Four Watchmen of Science in my book *From Mystery to Meaning*.[3] These assumptions are so fundamental to our thinking that nobody doubts them, yet none of them were considered necessarily true in the ancient and medieval worlds. The failure of Greek philosophers to grasp them probably delayed the progress of science for at least fifteen centuries. Indeed, ordinary life changed little from the time of Alexander the Great until the eighteenth century, except for the influence of gunpowder and the magnetic compass. Yet their beginnings can probably be traced back at least to Roger Bacon, two centuries before Columbus.

The first of these assumptions I have called the principle of *integrity*. We begin with the facts and follow the trail of truth wherever it may lead. No idea is too sacred, no law too certain to be immune from questioning or attack whenever there is adequate evidence. The history of science is littered with theories and beliefs which could not stand under the weight of later discoveries. Even Newton's law of gravity has had to be modified under Einstein's attack. There was a time when the Bible was considered the final word in science as well as religion, and many a man died or was imprisoned for questioning the current interpretation of Genesis. Yet the battle has been largely won in the fields of physical and biological science, in spite of some conservative Protestant groups.

The second of these assumptions is *causation*, that is, that behind everything there must be a cause or a combination of causes which is adequate in position, in power and in character to account for it. Most of us are positive that the principle of cause and effect is universal, forgetting that for most of the world's history men believed in magic, results without an adequate cause, or in miracle, a supernatural suspension of normal causation. Believe it or not, Arabian Nights and the black magic of the Middle Ages once represented the sober beliefs of most men and women. Thus some 300,000 women died in witchcraft persecutions during three centuries.

The corollary of this is the postulate of *uniformity*. We are most of us convinced beyond a shadow of doubt that the world makes sense, that the same combination of causes can always be depended on to give the same result, though we recognize that different combinations may also give identical results. Thus two plus two is always four, but four may also be the sum of one and three, or the product of four times one. The observed uniformities of nature we call laws, but they are actually nothing but a short-hand statement of principles we have come to trust through numerous observations, and with no exceptions. Any confirmed exception requires that a more general statement be formulated to include it. The assumptions of causation and uniformity do away with all magic and miracle in the modern world, though the heart of man still hankers after them as is witnessed by the current popularity of astrology and palmistry.

The fourth assumption, which is fundamental to the scientific method, is that there must be a process or linkage between cause and effect. It may be mechanical, chemical, electrical, or even logical and statistical, when the physical linkage is unknown or cannot be observed. We are certain that it has to be present wherever there is a cause and effect relationship or even consistently parallel phenomena. We do not have to be sure in which direction the process is moving, or it may be reversible, but the scientific mind insists that the connection is there. This assumption is so fundamental that there is no commonly used word to describe it.

These four assumptions underlie all scientific thinking and its development in the modern world, although they are rarely all recognized and stated except by philosophers. Yet each one of them is essential to our study of the waiting world and will be referred to as the *Four Watchmen* — integrity, causation, uniformity and linkage.

Now there is not the slightest reason why these four principles have to be restricted in their application to the physical world, which can be weighed, measured, or counted. This is indeed a fundamental fallacy of our twentieth-century thinking, an assumption which has frozen spiritual research while facilitating material progress, a dogma which has provided boundless physical wealth while leaving us in the Middle Ages as far as spiritual understanding is concerned. When these four postulates are accepted as valid for research in the non-physical world of spirit, we may expect a comparable increase in spiritual understanding and power. Let us see how they apply.

The principle of integrity rightly persuades us that no physical roads for the possible prevention or cure of cancer should be left unexplored. It would seem to be just as true for psychological and spiritual controls such as faith and prayer, and even disposition. If it is right for a psychiatrist to study the dreams of his patient for an understanding of his behavior or moods, should it not be just as proper and essential to study visions or deathbed experiences for hints about the reality and nature of a possible life beyond the body? To be stopped by creeds, threats, personal prejudice or public opinion from honestly examining any field is as unscientific and dangerous as the inquisition or witchcraft in the seventeenth century.

When the postulate of causation is applied to material like that in Chapter I, we search for rational explanations. If the stories stood by themselves without supporting evidence it might be possible to claim, for example, that they are products of dreams, fantasy, wishful thinking and even deceit. However, they are but samples of hundreds, often with strongly supporting evidence, some of which have been discussed in earlier chapters. More than that, they come independently from many sources, very often to the great surprise of those who experience them, and tend to corroborate each other in the picture they present. Their most obvious explanation is that they represent trustworthy experiences with a world of reality beyond the reach of our normal physical senses. It is easy to dismiss these stories as superstition or imagination with a shrug of the shoulders and a wave of the hand, but not if we are looking for adequate explanations for their original meaning. With each story and type of experience, the presumption for the reality of the waiting world becomes stronger. In the absence of any other adequate theory or explanation — and I know of none — we become most unscientific when we deny the obvious truth.

The third postulate of uniformity, that is, of dependability, at first hardly seems to apply to the spontaneous phenomena which form the bulk of our data in this study. Obviously it is impossible to set up tests for their validity, or to reproduce them at will. Only by examining large numbers of cases, comparing them and finding common patterns, it is possible to begin to form pictures which may bear some resemblance to the reality we may expect to experience when our time comes to die. People are beginning to do this, for example: the deathbed observations of Dr Karlis Osis, and the out-of-the-body experiences by Celia Green. More significant is the work of Dr Robert Crookall in analyzing large numbers of incidents on the assumption that there is an orderly and dependable waiting world, and that its principles may be found. Without doubt many of his conclusions, which were discussed in Chapter VII, will have to be modified as the field is more carefully explored. Yet the fact remains that the scientific assumption of orderliness when applied to the study of death is at last beginning to open the doors of understanding, through which the myths of primitive man, the insights of the mystics and the collected experiences of man today may all unite to present a promise of a life beyond the body, glorious beyond the dreams of the past.

It is the assumption of linkage between cause and effect that seems most difficult to apply to the non-physical phenomena of our study. This has probably been the greatest obstacle both to the commonsense and the scientific acceptance of our data as trustworthy. Here was the cause of the greatest quarrel with the psychologists, who could not conceive of any process or linkage between cause and apparent effect in J. B. Rhine's statistical studies of ESP. Therefore they would not even examine his evidence. However, it should be noted that science itself does not reject physical phenomena just because it cannot identify the inter-relationships which are assumed to be involved. A prime example is the mechanism of gravity. This has never been discovered, although the theory of relativity may ultimately unlock this secret. Just how the forces which hold the planets together in space actually operate is a problem that remains to tantalize science. Both in physics and biology there are many cases in which no physical link has so far been discovered yet where causal relations are obvious.

The discoveries of atomic physics and the nature of the electromagnetic spectrum are breaking the impasse between the physical and the psychic. The realization that matter is not solid, but that for the human body, for example, it is of the order of one $1:5000^3$ solid, is bringing a new humility to the men of science, and opening new vistas for the study of the world of spirit and of life beyond the body. This means that if a body could be compressed to the density of the nucleus of an atom, all three billion human bodies on the face of the earth could be put in a two-quart jar, with room left over! Thus many levels of reality, vibration or density may exist in the same space without interfering with each other and without our being aware of them. On the same way there are a great many different wavelengths from TV and radio stations available in any one spot, but only by tuning one in and all others out can we translate them into pictures or music on a physical level.

If this is true for the material world as we now experience it, the way is open to understand and accept the possibility of other realms of existence all about and within us. The body of the Risen Christ appearing and disappearing through closed doors is no longer an obstacle to belief. Telepathy and clairvoyance no longer seem so impossible now that space-ships transmit movies from the moon for worldwide viewing. The fantastic reports coming through the radio telescope and the cyclotron about galaxies and atomic particles make Jules Verne and Alice in Wonderland seem *passé* and the stories told in Chapter I tame in comparison. The speculations of sober physicists and astronomers are stranger than science fiction. Combine the inner world of the mind, the com-plexities of the atom, and the probability of billions of planets not too different from our earth, along with a sprinkling of relativity — all of these the products of this generation of science — and the result is a climate as ready to accept other worlds of reality as the Middle Ages were to believe the magic of Merlin or the prophecies of Nostradamus. Thus the back of traditional materialism has been broken by science itself.

However, even in these days of instant communication and rapidly changing ideas the traditional battle between science and religion continues. Viewpoints are hardened into pre-judice, so it is difficult for the working scientist along with the great mass of people to realize that the war is over and that it is once more respectable to have a soul. Sir Arthur Eddington, one of the greatest of recent cosmological astronomers, is said to have remarked that the more closely the universe is examined the more it looks like a gigantic thought. Under these conditions more thinking people are beginning to accept the approach proposed in this book, and many are reporting their own personal experiences and spec-ulations about the nature of the spiritual life and the waiting world. So it can now be said that science is no longer the enemy of research outside physical realms, but rather provides the logical techniques and basic assumptions for valid experimentation and speculation.

The work of Professor Harold Burr at Yale Medical School and recently reported experiments in plant psychology have broken down the old physical limitations of the scientific method and pointed the way toward a larger and more inclusive study of mankind in which the grave is not the end, but a new beginning. Some years ago Professor Burr began to present evidence of the possible existence of fields of force surrounding all living organisms. These varied with the species, and even with the health of the specimen, but they disappeared at death. He did this with a micro-voltmeter sensitive to as little as a millionth of a volt of electricity. In 1932 he announced as a working hypothesis "an underlying electric dynamic field whose characteristic forces impose patterns on protoplasm". This would seem to require a rethinking of the philosophy of biology, because it means that the form of physical life is controlled not by the genetic pattern, but by something neither physical nor chemical. The implications of this, confirmed by more recent experiments, can hardly be exaggerated.

More amazing and just as significant are the reports of the experiments of lie-detector expert Cleve Backster with vines and certain animals in his office, as reported in *National Wildlife* and other magazines in 1969. Almost accidentally he discovered that a philodendron to which his polygraph (lie detector) was attached responded violently to his decision to burn a leaf. He could not believe that plants could respond to human thoughts and animal emotions, and only after three years of investigation did he permit the publication of his still tentative conclusions. As F. L. Kunz says in *Main Currents,* "One of the conclusions Backster has reached is that, staggering as it may be to contemplate, a life signal may connect all creation."

It may well be that the time is drawing near when men of science will lead the way toward a new day of faith by the very logic of their discoveries that the nature of life is non-physical in essence. Then indeed our debt to them will be doubled as mankind is freed to explore scientifically and logically their nature and destiny.

11 The Bible—Shackle or Spur?

The Bible itself and its various interpretations which have become a part of traditional theology form the biggest religious obstacle to the study and understanding of the life beyond death by the average man. Just as we had to examine the assumptions, true and false, of modern science and then apply them to out-of-this-world phenomena, so also must we consider various attitudes toward the Bible and its authority before our witnesses for the waiting world can be fairly judged by many Christians. Here, too, we may find not only encouragement for our investigation, but also some unexpected confirmations and guidelines.

There are two strains of teaching and belief in the Bible which have largely shackled progress in all forms of psychic research among Christian people in the past. One of these is the repeated condemnation of communication with the dead in the Old Testament as illustrated by the story of King Saul and the woman of Endor. Any such contact was supposed to be a form of idolatry, and is interpreted by many today as demon worship. I have had friends and relatives plead with me with tears to give up all investigation in this field lest I find myself condemned to the fires of hell. It was one of the unmentionables in my childhood, along with sex and perversion.

The other scriptural idea blocking our pursuit of this path is the belief that the so-called New Testament theology of the resurrection and future judgement invalidates anything that research may claim to discover. It is possible that the opposite is true; that is, that the results of careful investigation may force a rewriting of some of our theology. Actually, there are several theories about the future, each supposed to be the true biblical teaching according to their particular proponents, although we will give attention primarily to that of the resurrection after sleeping in our graves until Christ comes again. Even the slight consideration we can give in this chapter may show that none of these can be accepted to the exclusion of all others, and that there are indications of still other viewpoints which point toward a richer and more trustworthy faith.

Before examining this biblical material in more detail, it will be necessary to ask again what we mean by the Bible being the word of God. The idea that every word is literally true is so obviously false that we need not belabor the matter. For the present discussion the fact that there are mutually contradictory teachings about the next life, as we shall be considering them, is sufficient evidence. Yet popular fundamentalism claims that if we question a single word, then none of the Bible is to be trusted. What do the sanitary regulations of Leviticus, or the conflicting genealogies of Jesus, or the social customs of the Hellenic world which still compel women to wear hats in some churches, have to do with life in the twentieth century? Commands to massacre and blessings on murder are both there along with orders to eat no pork and to stone blasphemers. What a book!

Yet we may rightly feel that it does contain the word of God, a progressive revelation of his nature and purpose, climaxed by the life and teachings of Jesus who so embodied the divine nature that to this day men feel that they best know God by knowing him. But even of Jesus it was written that he "increased in wisdom and strength, and in favor with God and man". Actually we can take the Bible as the word of God only by thinking of it as a book of religion, and interpreting each part of it in the light of the life and character of the Master. While he knew and loved the Old Testament, he did not hesitate to quote it six times in one chapter of his most famous sermon, and then to contradict it each time with his "but I say unto you". (Matthew 5)

For practical purposes even the fundamentalist does the same, either skipping or giving allegorical interpretations of sub-Christian or statements that are obviously false in the light of today's knowledge. Few today doubt that the world is round, yet Galileo was imprisoned for suggesting it in a period when men were sure that the Bible taught that the earth was flat and the sun moved from east to west. As long as we take the Bible as true word for word it will continue to shackle any honest study of many of the basic questions of the human heart. But it may be that when we study it honestly and seriously, the Bible will be changed from blinders over our eyes to a spur to deeper exploration of those things that Jesus could not tell his disciples because they were not yet able to accept or understand them (John 16:12).

Now as to the command (Deuteronomy 18:10-11, American translation) to have nothing to do with psychical research: "There must not be found among you anyone who makes his son or daughter pass through fire, a diviner, a soothsayer, an auger, a sorcerer, a charmer, a medium, a magician, or a necromancer." These practices were all associated with the pagan worship of their neighbors and were thus condemned. Equally good reasons could be advanced for being cautious about trusting astrology or palmistry today. Yet in Chapter VI we saw that the origins or prophecy go back to some of the same practices. So might it be said that while both the law and the prophets condemned them the prophets actually converted them to the service of an ethical religion.

As mentioned above, King Saul is reported to have enforced this law, but after the death of Samuel, a prophet and his adviser, he himself consulted a medium, simply called a woman of Endor (not a 'witch' as in the King James headings). The story puts the woman in a very good light. At great personal danger she agreed to help the disguised king in his extremity, asking no fee and giving him a fine meal when she realized how distraught he was. There is no criticism at all of the woman, although 1 Chronicles 10:13-14 is often quoted to the effect that God killed Saul for going to her instead of seeking "guidance from the Lord". It is interesting to note in 1 Samuel 28:6 that before Saul went to the woman he had already "inquired of the Lord" in three ways — by dreams, Urim (a means of divination) and prophets — without getting any satisfaction. And as to his death, 1

Samuel 31:4 says he committed suicide and 2 Samuel 1:10 that he was killed by an Amalekite. The most that may be drawn from all this is that nothing can be concluded, and that the Old Testament cannot be taken word for word as true.

This story does have one value for us in being one of the earliest records of mediumship. It is thoroughly compatible with modern experience, and is a fine example of a gifted 'sensitive' comparable to many of the best known in Europe and America in the last two generations. The woman was not a sorceress or a witch, yet it is out of this background of misinterpretation and superstition that much of the present-day opposition to the investigation of the next world stems.

In view of the Hebrew prophets' strong and repeated condemnation of mediumship and other forms of possible contact with another world, it is not surprising that they had less faith and concern about the future life than many other primitive races. Mediumship, or communication with the dead, naturally carries with it strong assurances that life continues after death, but when practices that would strengthen that belief are forbidden it is only natural that such a faith should wither. So Jehovah was considered a national God, guiding and guarding his chosen people. The rewards for virtue and obedience were all in this life: financial success, a long life, and many descendants for the individual; prosperity and freedom for the nation as a whole. They did not often go as far as the Preacher in Ecclesiastes quoted in the Introduction, but 2 Samuel 14:14 states the general attitude: "We must all die, we are like water spilt on the ground, which cannot be gathered up again."

However, they could not actually conceive of extinction, but rather thought of Sheol as the next thing to it, as described in the Psalm 88, verses 3-6 and 10-12:

> For my soul is full of troubles,
>   and my life draws near to Sheol.
> I am reckoned among those who go down to the Pit;
>   I am a man who has no strength,
> like one forsaken among the dead,
>   like the slain that lie in the grave,

like those whom thou dost remember no more,
    for they are cut off from thy hand.
Thou hast put me in the depths of the Pit,
    in the regions dark and deep.

Dost thou work wonders for the dead?
    Do the shades rise up to praise thee?
Is thy steadfast love declared in the grave,
    or thy faithfulness in Abaddon?
Are thy wonders known in the darkness,
    or thy saving help in the land of forgetfulness?

No wonder all rewards had to be in this life! Until after the Babylonian captivity there is little hint of anything more. Such passages as Isaiah 26:19 refer to national life, and the last words of Psalms 16 and 23 could probably be translated best *as long as I live* even though different Hebrew words are used. "If a man die shall he live again?" and the quotations from Psalm 88 are rhetorical questions to which the answer is "Of course not." This general belief continued even after the time of Jesus. Thus the Sadducees who formed the conservative priestly party did not believe in the future life or a physical resurrection. On this basis they naturally cooperated with their Roman rulers as the only reasonable way for sensible men, and were therefore kept in power as the Sanhedrin and High Priest by them.

On the other hand, some of the captives in the Persian period were stimulated to new ways of thinking by their contacts with Zoroastrianism. Apart from Judaism, this was the noblest faith of the ancient world, so some of the returning refugees brought back with them developed beliefs in a hierarchy of angels and demons and a physical resurrection from their graves when the Messiah should come and set up his perfect kingdom. Their moral code with its motto, "I profess good thoughts, good words and good deeds" is nearer to the Sermon on the Mount than the older Hebrew ideals.

These ideas were increasingly naturalized or adopted into popular religion as time went on, especially during the long periods of foreign rule. This became the popular "fundamentalism" of the common people: specifically that a descendant of David would appear as a military leader and restore their kingdom to its ancient glory. Those who had already died would share in it through the resurrection. Needless to say, they never accommodated themselves to Greek or Roman rule, but were always ready to revolt with the slightest encouragement. Scholars are divided as to whether the name Pharisee really means a separatist or a Persian. It sounds suspiciously like Parsee, as the modern followers of Zoroaster are called in India. Whether they were nicknamed Pharisees (like modern Methodists and Quakers) because of their rigid ideas or their Persian origin is not important, but it is clear that they maintained their intense Jewish nationalism against all comers even when scattered across the eastern Mediterranean world.

So it was with Saul, who later became the Apostle Paul. Though he was born in Tarsus, a city in Asia Minor hundreds of miles from Palestine, he was trained as a strict Pharisee in the school of Gamaliel (Acts 22:3), and believed in the resurrection, angels and spirits (23:6-8). When he became a Christian he retained his old theology, simply reinterpreting it to include Jesus as the expected Messiah and the first example of the resurrection. This is brought out most clearly in 1st and 2nd Thessalonians and 1 Corinthians 15, although in the latter his emphasis was beginning to change. Throughout his earlier ministry he taught that the dead sleep in their graves until Christ shall come again and set up his eternal kingdom. He is so positive and clear in his statements, and so persuasive in his argument, that anybody who accepts his letters as literally inspired is more or less compelled to believe likewise.

Jesus was almost certainly brought up on Pharisaic ideas, and he used much of its vocabulary even when expressing contrary conclusions. His early proclamation of the coming kingdom, following the lead of John the Baptist and many of his parables and sayings, reflects their viewpoint even when he was critical of them. For example, the reading from Isaiah 61 in the synagogue at Nazareth (Luke 4:18-20) is a perfect statement of their hope, but he stopped just before the climax from their standpoint, omitting "and the day of vengeance of our God".

When the Sadducees tried to trap him with a question about a woman with seven husbands he went out of his way to state the survival of death instead of a future resurrection. Abraham, Isaac and Jacob are not dead, waiting to be raised up in their old bodies. This is very different from sleeping in their graves, whatever that means (see Luke 20:27-38). Even more important was the transfiguration appearance of Moses and Elijah to Jesus and three of his disciples, not only because it demonstrated that the dead are actually alive, but also because it showed that Jesus did not take seriously the strong Old Testament prohibition of any contact with the dead. Just as King Saul went to a medium when he was in a desperate situation, so did Jesus consult the dead when he was facing the idea of having to die on a cross. He received the answer and strength which he needed when Moses and Elijah talked with him about "his departure which he was to accomplish at Jerusalem" (Luke 9:31).

It is interesting to note how Jesus' action fits in with the advice given in 1 John 4:1: "Do not believe every spirit, but test the spirits to see whether they are of God." The next two verses give the method of testing: did the spirits confess that Christ had come in the flesh? Although this hardly seems a reliable test in view of the recognition of Jesus by evil spirits (Mark 1:24 and 5:8, for example), it clearly involved the early church in spirit communication. More than this, one of the gifts of the spirit as given in 1 Corinthians 12:10 is "the ability to distinguish between spirits". Glossolalia, or speaking in tongues, which has had such a resurgence in recent years, is also considered by many people to be a form of spirit communication. All of this makes it fairly certain that the early Christians felt that they were free to make whatever contact they could with the dead, and that they had the example of their Master and his disciples in so doing.

Now the Apostle Paul did not know Jesus in the body, but all the same he wrote the earliest Christian theology in terms of his own Pharisaic beliefs. This included the soon coming of Jesus and the dead rising again. For example in 1 Corinthians 7:26 he urged young folks not to get married because of the "impending distress" that would precede Christ's reappearance for "we shall all be changed, in a moment, in a twinkling of an eye, at the last trumpet. For the trumpet will sound and the dead will be raised imperishable." (15:51-52) This faith dominated the early church for at least a generation, even though it was not taught by Jesus.

At every time of great crisis in history since the first century, there has been a revival of Adventism, that is, a belief in the imminent return of Christ. The period beginning with World War I in 1914 has been the time of greatest change in all history, with more uncertainty, destruction and starvation than was ever conceived possible. It has likewise seen the greatest revival of this faith, not only among conservative and Adventist movements, but by scholars such as Charles Whiston of the (Episcopal) Church Divinity School of the Pacific, and Oscar Cullman, who delivered the 1955 lecture at Harvard University on the immortality of man.[1] Both men take the position that theirs is *the* New Testament faith, and that current ideas of immortality and heaven have been borrowed from Greek philosophy. Strangely, they both forget that Jesus condemned their doctrine after having its falsity demonstrated on the Mount of Transfiguration. Nor is there any supporting evidence of its truth either in history or present-day research. Still this old Persian theory continues to cast its spell over the minds of men, especially when they find it difficult to face the problems and difficulties of twentieth-century life.

Now as we look at Paul's letters in the order they were presumably written it is clear how the emphasis changes. The return of Christ and the resurrection dominate the two letters to the Thessalonians, but they are of secondary importance in the next three (Romans, Galatians and 1 Corinthians), although he still expects Jesus to reappear in his lifetime. Then between writing 1st and 2nd Corinthians, Paul had a very difficult time and despaired of his life. So in 2 Corinthians 1:9 and 5:6-8 he anticipates his own death and going to live with Christ.

When we come to 12:2-4 we find a passage most interesting from our standpoint. He has been defending himself as an apostle and giving his qualifications, and then goes on to say, "I know a man in Christ who fourteen years ago was caught up to the third heaven — whether in the body or out of the body I do not know, God knows. And I know that this man was caught up into paradise . . . and heard things that cannot be told, which man may not utter." All scholars are agreed that here Paul is referring to himself, but it is not clear whether he is describing two experiences, or only one. Now this had taken place fourteen years previously, but if it is true that he saw into heaven, then his concept of the dead as sleeping must be false. He had apparently never thought of the inconsistency; nor is there any certainty that he thought about it even later.

However, the next three letters to churches — Philippians, Colossians and Ephesians — were all written in prison when Paul had plenty of time to think, and they all contain theological differences from his previous writings so great that some scholars think that he could not have been the author. While Philippians has three and Colossians one passing reference to the return of Christ, each of them puts far from emphasis upon his greatness and glory, Ephesians approaching the prologue of John in grandeur as he describes the cosmic pre-existent Christ (see Philippians 2:6-11, Colossians 1:15-20, Ephesians 1:3-10, 19-32). All of them carry an assurance of the heavenly life immediately after death without waiting for a future resurrection on earth, and claim that ultimately the love and power of Christ is so great "that at the name of Jesus every knee should bow, in heaven and on earth and under the earth, and every tongue confess that Jesus Christ is Lord to the glory of God the Father." (Philippians 2:10-11) "For in him all the fullness of God was pleased to dwell, and through him to reconcile to himself all things, whether on earth or in heaven." (Colossians 1:19-20)

Now this is pure universalism, that is, the doctrine that every soul will ultimately be saved. It points back to Jesus the Good Shepherd who seeks the lost sheep until he finds every last one of them whether in this life or the world to come, who prayed for those who were crucifying him, "Father, forgive them for they know not what they do," and who promised the thief on the cross, "Today thou shalt be with me in paradise." As previously noted, Paul did not know Jesus physically, nor of his interpretation of the resurrection and the unlimited forgiveness of God; but out of his long fellowship with the living Christ he finally came to the same understanding. If either he had realized these things earlier and had not been so blinded by his legalistic Pharisaic theology, or had explained how he had changed his mind, it would have saved centuries of unchristian debate. But Paul wrote these warm, vital and up-to-date letters, always giving in unforgettable terms his latest understanding of the meaning of Christ for the world.

The confusion caused by these conflicting ideas of the future is nowhere better illustrated than by the incompatible and contradictory inferences in one of the committals found until recently in the Episcopal and Methodist funeral rituals:

Forasmuch as the spirit of the departed hath returned to the God who gave it, we therefore commit his body to the ground, earth to earth, ashes to ashes, dust to dust, looking for the general resurrection in the last day, and the life of the world to come, through our Lord Jesus Christ; at whose coming in glorious majesty to judge the world, the earth and the sea shall give up their dead; and the corruptible bodies of those who sleep in him shall be changed and made like unto his glorious body . . .

It is hard to imagine a bigger bundle of irreconcilable phrases in one sentence. "The spirit hath returned to the God who made it" and "the life of the world to come" belong to one tradition; while "the general resurrection in the last day", "at whose coming in glorious majesty to judge the world", "the earth and the sea shall give up their dead", and "the corruptible bodies of those who sleep in him shall be changed and made like unto his glorious body" give an entirely different and much more vivid picture. How much, even today, we need to be straightened out in this matter of the waiting world!

There is no reason to discuss the many other interpretations of New Testament statements about the next world. It is the revival of Adventist theories of the end of the world which has posed the largest New Testament obstacle to a scientific investigation of possible evidence, and which therefore had to be described and answered. Many Christians and Jews of varying theological persuasion also opposed it because of the Mosaic taboos already discussed. The early church fathers, such as Tertullian and Origen, could not conceive of an endless hell, or that most Christians were ready for a perfect heaven. Indeed, the idea of everlasting torture was not emphasized by the church until after the year 500.[2] Thus the church gradually developed the belief in Purgatory as preparation for heaven, and in prayers for the dead to speed them on their way.

The Protestant Reformation was partly a revolt against the selling of indulgences as advance payment for sins as a means of raising money. As a consequence Protestants have generally opposed prayers for the dead, but rather have believed in an immediate judgement after death at which the soul is either rewarded with an endless heaven or tortured forever in hell. Neither of these theories takes adequate account of the moral differences between individuals or the character of a Christ-like God, although the Catholic teaching is preferable — when cleansed of its extremes.

Yet both Jesus and Paul seem to point toward a gospel which is good news for all mankind. If the persistent love of God does not outlast all of the stubborn resistance of men then God is not all-powerful. The conditional immortality suggested by John 3:16, "For God so loved the world that he gave his only Son, that whoever believes in him should not perish, but have eternal life" and Romans 6:23, "For the wages of sin is death, but the free gift of God is eternal life in Christ Jesus our Lord," leaves God ultimately defeated. Not one soul can be left out in the end. It will be interesting to see what confirmations research gives to this.

The problem is that there are no hints in the Bible as to how these things can be in terms of our modern scientific world view. The visions of John in the book of Revelations are so dramatic and symbolic that they carry a great sense of urgency, but not of reality. That the church was quickly aware of the problem is suggested in 1 Peter (3:9 and 4:6) that Jesus preached to the dead, and by a reference to baptism for the dead in 1 Corinthians 15:29. During the Dark Ages the primary obsession was to escape hell, and later came the allegories of Dante, Milton and Bunyan, and legends like Faust and Mephistopheles. Then came the Inquisition and the witchcraft persecutions, followed by great revivals, much of them based on the preaching of hellfire and brimstone. Thus there has been little relation to reality in the doctrines of the life beyond death throughout Christian history. Likewise there has been comparatively little intelligent discussion of it in religious circles, either orthodox or liberal, in recent years.

So the traditional doctrines have lost much of their hold in this century because of the new science with its gifts and gadgets, and nothing has come to take their place. Yet there is probably just as great a concern as ever. The leaders of a large meeting of college students in the United Presbyterian Church some time in the 1960s were obviously disconcerted when the students chose immortality as the subject they wanted to be discussed.

What may be concluded from this brief study of the Bible, in relation to a world which may be waiting for us at death? Here are some suggestions:

The ancient Mosaic taboo against all forms of contact with the dead was disobeyed by Jesus and the early church; nor does it have any authority today. The early Hebrews were largely agnostic and negative about the future life, generally believing in an impersonal Sheol or Hades. Persian resurrection theories found their way with some of the returning captives after the Babylonian captivity, and re-appeared among the Pharisees of Jesus' time. They are also heard among Adventists today, but are without religious authority or research support. The final conclusions of Jesus and Paul are compatible with both modern speculation and research.

Thus the Bible no longer need be a shackle binding us to the dogmas and fears of the past, but may be a spur to speculation, research and discovery in the most important field of human thought, if the race is to have the motivation and wisdom to solve the pressing social and ecological problems of the twentieth and twenty-first centuries.

12 Can This be True?

Can God tell a lie? Or the Pope be guilty of burglary? Or my wife commit murder? There are some things beyond my power to believe, no matter what the evidence might be. They are so contrary to what I already know that I would be sure there was something wrong with the witnesses or the evidence. Or in terms of our Watchmen of science, they would violate the principle of orderliness and dependability. If God, who is truth, could lie, then this is an insane world. So would it be if one plus one equalled one or orange trees grew bananas.

On this principle many readers may well have shut their minds to the testimony of our five witnesses. It does not jibe with the whole foundation of religion as it has been taught for almost two thousand years, or with the picture painted by science for at least a century. So I thought for half of my adult life. Therefore I refused to even examine the evidence, just as I would have refused to listen to gossip about my wife. Rather, I might have been tempted to resort to violence to stop such slander.

This was just what happened in the Inquisition. It was felt that heresy would lead some away from the truth on which life depended, and that it would be better for heretics to be burned at the stake than to cause others to burn in hell. They had Jesus behind them, too. "Whoever causes one of these little ones who believe in me to sin, it would be better for him if a great millstone were hung round his neck and he were thrown into the sea." (Mark 9:42) While these are gentler days, when physical violence against heretics is no longer permitted, there are many who feel just as strongly about those who present such interpretations of life. If words and looks would kill, I would long ago have explored these matters for myself in the next life. However, I am still much alive — and unrepentant still.

Instead of remaining on the defensive it would be better to notice how traditional teachings about the next life stand up when placed alongside the basic tenets of Christianity. We could be in for some surprises. When the life and teachings of Jesus are examined even casually, certain basic conclusions about the nature of God, or whatever is behind the universe, become clear. Our scientific assumptions assume that the world in its foundation character can be no less than its manifestations at their best. Man cannot rise higher than his Creator just as water cannot rise above its source. Result can never be greater than cause, but it can be less. We have discussed this earlier, and it only needs to be mentioned now, that whatever is behind human life, that is, God, must be as good or better than the best we know in human experience. This is to say that the unseen world can be no less than we see in Jesus of Nazareth. We have a self-contradiction which the man of science and of honest religion cannot endure if the principles of the life beyond cannot be reconciled with the best we know in this life on earth.

The great ideas that Jesus taught his disciples, and which he illustrated in his life, could be summarized as follows: God is love, and anything which is less than loving in our relation to either God or our brother man is sin and must be repented. Man is created in the spiritual image of God and is destined to freely grow into his character of perfect love. God is all-powerful within the limits of his loving purpose for man. God has revealed his wisdom, love and power in Jesus in order that man might fulfil his eternal destiny. This includes patience and forgiveness without limit.

These can be subdivided and modified, but they will stand up no matter how they are stated.

Now, how do the traditional teachings about the next world fit in with these four statements which are to be found throughout the teachings of Jesus, especially in the first three gospels? Without trying to summarize them in detail, because there are many varied schools of thought, there are several simple statements that can be made. Any theory which suggests that some souls will be forever lost is a denial either of the love, the power, or the wisdom of God, and is heresy indeed. Any theory that God's love and forgiveness is ever unavailable is a betrayal of Christ and of the unity of God. As Whittier put it, "We cannot drift beyond His love and care." Any teaching saying that God would torture a soul forever for any reason whatsoever makes a God a devil indeed. No parent will punish, nor judge condemn the innocent for the guilty. A God who does this is worse than any earthly parent or court and cannot be called God.

There are proof texts for all of these, yet they violate the very nature of God and of the human conscience which is His gift. Such texts are either due to faulty interpretation by His hearers or false transmissions. It is easier to mix oil and water than to fit traditional heaven and hell, or the revived Persian theories of death and resurrection into the character and teaching of Jesus. Heaven would be hell indeed for a mother whose son is forever beyond forgiveness and redemption. So would it be for God — unless we have confused him with our own devilment.

Now on the other hand, what contradictions are there between Jesus and the picture of the future given by our witnesses? I have been unable to find them. It is a continuation of this life in its essential moral and spiritual character. God still loves, and Christ still seeks to save. We have to live with ourselves until we are ready to change. Help and forgiveness are always offered. Can these things be? Once I felt that the old teachings were a logical and scientific monstrosity, and that the waiting world I have pictured could be nothing more than the figment of a disordered mind and no closer to reality than the man on the moon or the Wizard of Oz. Now that men have walked on the moon and computers can do more than any wizard I am ready to examine the evidence honestly and objectively. It seems to me that it stands up as well or better than atoms, relativity or evolution from a scientific standpoint, and as more nearly Christian from the biblical standpoint.

Perhaps those who still doubt should ask themselves three questions. First, at what points are my facts either faulty or false? To answer this question honestly one must go through a process of research as painstaking as the one I went through for twenty-five years, and then be willing to give an honest answer. Secondly, at what points does my analysis of the scientific method fall down, and where is my logic false? While it may be stated much better, and undoubtedly has flaws, I have not been able to find them. Thirdly, if the facts still stand and the logic is correct, what alternative interpretations of the waiting world are available? I know of none.

Can these things be? I do not know, but certainly the dice of research and scientific reasoning seem to be loaded in their favor, and I for one am willing to gamble on it. And how shall we gamble?

Let us pretend, like children, that these things *are* true, and that there is soon to open for each one of us a new world just waiting to be explored. It is a world of mystery and delight, a world of marvellous beauty and infinite truth, a world of glorious friendship and limitless potential, a world of sunrise and eternity.

And it may well all be true — better than our fondest dreams.

Adventuring in Bookland

"Of the making of books there is no end." From the Egyptian *Book of the Dead* to the latest paperback there are said to be some 300,000 dealing with life beyond the grave, extra-sensory perception, and related subjects, 75,000 of them in English. A considerable portion of all books of religion, including the Bible, would fall into this category, although comparatively few of them stay strictly within the limits of our subject.

Most of the older ones purport to be revelations from the gods, or are the work of priests and mystics without reference to acceptable evidence or scientific reasoning. Even in recent years the greater number, most of them privately printed, give the writers' individual experiences with the world beyond by means of automatic writing or some other form of ESP. It is easy to get hung up on one writer or viewpoint, especially when earnestly searching and unfamiliar with the great variety of experiences and interpretations, hence having no basis for discrimination. These books are indeed a jungle through which one may wander for years without finding a clear understanding or a firm foundation for faith.

Another type of book began to appear in the 1880s with the organization of the British and American Societies for Psychical Research. Each of these published such carefully documented annual reports of their investigations as to provide a valid basis for judgement by any serious student of the paranormal. They attracted some of the ablest scientific brains, including Sir William Barrett, Sir Oliver Lodge, Sir William Crookes, William James, Henri Bergson, L. P. Jacks and F. W. H. Myers, most of whom served a term as president and wrote books themselves of outstanding quality.

Two world wars and the resulting concern about death and its aftermath have brought an ever-increasing number of books representing every viewpoint and experience. Among them are masses of reports by scientists and religious leaders outlining their investigations in this field, and in most cases their conversion to faith in its validity.

However, the great body of orthodox scientific and religious authorities continues to reject the whole concept of ESP and of communication with the dead — whether they believe in personal survival or not. In many cases they substitute ridicule for any careful examination of the evidence. These books are not numerous, however, as it is far easier to support a positive view where one is emotionally involved than to fight a new movement. More numerous and widely circulated are those representing various branches of biblical fundamentalism. Most of these warn against any contact with mediumship as doing business with the devil or his emmisaries.

In this appendix I will sketch my own early adventures through this great literary jungle, putting up some signposts pointing to a few writers and books I have found most profitable, and likewise a few warnings against uncritical acceptance of others without careful evaluation. In many cases there are probably others just as good or even better than those which have come to my attention. If I missed your favorite I am probably the loser.

In 1941 I happened on a book by Professor J. B. Rhine of Duke University, *The Reach of the Mind,* in which he claimed to have proved by statistical methods that the mind had certain extra-sensory powers, specifically clairvoyance, telepathy and psychokinesis (the power to move objects by thought). I put it down in disgust feeling that Rhine was hopelessly unscientific. Then the thought occurred that he had simply given a report of his research, and that to reject his ideas without testing them was to call him a liar. The simplest test I could make was to try to influence the fall of dice by my thought. It really did not occur to me that it could be done, but the first hour of tests gave such fantastic results that I could have won any crap game in the country three times over. Over a period of several months it was a million to one that my results could be coincidence! My old world of scientific materialism had begun to crumble, and I started into the jungle.

Of course Rhine did not deal at all with the survival of personality after death, but the ice had been broken and I began to take a new look at a number of things that my liberal theology had led me to doubt, especially miracles, intercessory prayer and immortality. Previously I had turned away from anything in this field as being below the dignity of any intelligent man. I still remember my sinking feeling when I stumbled onto *The Betty Book* by Stewart Edward White. He was one of my favorite boyhood writers, and to think that he had let me down by falling for such superstition! How could he! But I have had to eat my thoughts. In the years since I have read all seven of the *Betty Books* and number them among the best popular reports of mediumship, although written in his easy-flowing fictional style.

So now I wandered through the jungle as chance or fancy led me, not at first trying to distinguish between fact and fiction. Much I read as science fiction, remembering, however, that many fantastic ideas of Jules Verne and Edward Bellamy are now sober facts of the space age. So also many of the ideas and viewpoints I once considered pure fantasy are now in the list of the possibly true. Others, such as stories of the islands of Mu and Atlantis, and the fields of astrology, palmistry and fortune-telling in general, I still take with many grains of salt. They are interesting if taken casually in small amounts, but very dangerous if swallowed in large doses.

Another large group of books were similar to the stories of exploration and hunting of my boyhood, except that they told of the personal experiences of those primarily concerned with inner space and the strange world of psychic phenomena. The plots were almost always the same, just as in 'whodunits' or westerns, except that the hero has discovered that he possesses a new key to life in some form of contact with the non-physical world of spirits, most often through the ouija board or automatic writing. This he feels impelled to share with the world, usually through a privately printed or subsidized book. The first few of these I found interesting, but their drab sameness soon palled, and I learned to pass them by very quickly. They all contain revelations of the next world — even as does this book — and the writer percipient, or medium, as the case may be, is certain that nobody else in history has ever had such a revelationary experience. Except for the conspiracy of silence on the part of traditional religion and education, most of the writers would have known of many other similar books, and so might have exercised a suitable restraint in giving theirs to the world.

Yet, by their very sameness and numbers these books have a great value which I did not realize for a long time. Where one or two witnesses tell a strange story which is doubted by the community at large, and which both pastors and scientists are sure is false, then it is unlikely that their stories will carry much weight. If those were the facts in the case I most surely would not be writing this. However, when there are literally hundreds of witnesses, in most cases unknown to each other, all giving similar testimony, the strength of their common report becomes almost irresistible. Of course if their statements were exactly alike collusion would be rightly assumed. But as it is, even one witness who was present, that is, who has had an experience revealing some facet of life beyond death, is more to be believed than a dozen authorities who are sure that it is impossible.

All the weight of ecclesiastical and scientific authority was against the possibility of Columbus finding either a new or the old world by sailing west in 1492. But after his return any illiterate sailor on any one of his caravels knew more than all the rest of the world put together. He had been there! So with the great number who tell their stories of the waiting world. They have been there and their tales agree as closely as do those who have witnessed an auto wreck.

As I look over the hundred or so books on the chest beside my table as I write I notice a great number dealing with reincarnation. Although that is not the subject of this book the growing popular interest in it is very evident. Many of the writers professed absolute disbelief in it a few years ago, but have been forced to change their tune through experience, logic, or, in some cases, by the growth of public acceptance. At least 75 per cent of the writers combine their acceptance of reincarnation with their faith in immortality. The result is that it is not possible to make any considerable literary study of personal survival without having to examine it. However, that is no reason why we should allow ourselves to get lost or sidetracked as we wander through the jungle.

We may likewise be tempted to stray from our goal by the many esoteric and occult books, those on mysticism and oriental philosophy, or those published by certain churches or schools of thought, usually centering on some modern master or prophet. All of these have their values and disciples. Any one of them, without the others, might seem to be God's new word for this generation, but all together they point in the same direction we are going.

So also do a large collection of new books by reporters and journalists who have jumped on the bandwagon. Some of these have discovered that they themselves have extra-sensory powers, and all of them have apparently been converted as a result of their own research. These books have usually been well researched, are generally reliable and consistent, and deal with many types of dramatic experience, most of them related to death and the future. All of them have been published by standard publishers, and some have become best sellers. The best can usually be purchased in paperback editions in drug stores and on newstands. I find them stimulating and thrilling, yet withal lacking in spiritual depth. From that standpoint they are both a challenge and a threat to the serious seeker after ultimate meanings. The best at hand are by Ruth Montgomery, Jess Stearn, Allen Spraggett, DeWitt Miller, Martin Ebon, Susy Smith, and Brad Steiger. Of a slightly different nature are some older ones by Alson Smith, Harold Sherman and Louisa Rhine. Nor should the biographies of Edgar Cayce by Thomas Sugrue and Gina Cerminara, nor of Arthur Ford, be omitted. All of these may serve to break through our traditional prejudices and create a sense of childlike wonder and anticipation which are first steps toward spiritual growth. At least this was my experience.

Even more surprising to me in my wanderings through bookland has been the discovery of books by religious leaders whom I trust, most of whom wrote only after retirement from the active ministry. The outstanding ones were by Sherwood Eddy and Leslie Weatherhead, both of whom I have quoted in sermons throughout my ministry. Without their honest and courageous examples I probably would not have ventured publicly into this field. Others with varied ecclesiastical backgrounds who have helped smooth my pathway are Ralph Harlow (Congregational), Johannes Greber (Roman Catholic), Horace Westwood (Unitarian), Margueritte Bro (Disciples), and more recently, Bishop James A. Pike (Episcopal).

Often in my explorations I have found a writer whose work has set the bells ringing in my mind, and started me off again to explore with greater enthusiasm and joy. Above all others I would name Raynor C. Johnson, an atomic physicist who was Master of Queen's College, University of Melbourne, in Australia, and who in retirement has produced half a dozen books of such spiritual depth, scientific persuasiveness and literary beauty that I turn back to them repeatedly for both guidance and inspiration. If I had to choose only one of his books the choice would be between the first and the most recent, *The Imprisoned Splendor* and *A Religious Outlook for Modern Man.*

I have quoted three other scientists who have moved into this field more often than any other writers. While there is basic agreement between them, they come from three centuries and represent very different approaches to our problem. Emanuel Swedenborg, an eighteenth-century scientist, inventor and civil servant, had a vision at the age of fifty-seven, after which he was able to visit the heavenly realms in semi-trance, and to report back what he had learned in numerous volumes.

A century and a half later, F. W. H. Myers, classical scholar and poet, made the first and greatest scientific study of death and survival. For a number of years following his death in 1901, several mediums received what purported to be messages from him through automatic writing. These are accepted by many scholars, including Raynor Johnson and Leslie Weatherhead, as among the best and probably most accurate accounts we have as to what we may expect after death. I have chosen two of these to use as I wrote.

More recently Dr Robert Crookall has assembled half a dozen volumes on death and related subjects, and is currently working on a number of others. His method is to gather great numbers of illustrations, often from sources which would otherwise be by-passed, and then to analyze them for similarities and differences, on which he bases his conclusions. His volumes are among the most significant published in this field during the 1960s.

As I scan the books beside me I count some three dozen other authors, many of whom have thrilled me with their stories and inspired me to continue my search. A few of them have been quoted along the way, but most of these will have to remain unacknowledged even though my debt to them is great. Without them this book would probably not have been written. Then there are literally hundreds of others I have borrowed and returned, or have scanned in libraries great and small. Such is the jungle, some would say jumble, of books waiting to be explored. Or it may be termed a treasure house which any who are both curious and courageous may explore. A warning: "Don't touch it if you are afraid of being shaken by a new approach to the deep mysteries of life," as Kirby Page once wrote about an earlier book of mine.

One by-product of my adventuring in bookland, or through this great jungle, was the restoration of much of the Bible to me. Many pages which once I read without really believing came alive to me as I realized that many strange tales of miracle and magic in both Testaments were actually being repeated today in the living experiences of ordinary men and women. The locale and the vocabulary may be different, but spiritual verities and psychic capacities continue from age to age the same. The Bible writers related them for the same reasons that they are to be found in many a modern book: they are true, they are not common, and they are very significant. Now that I know that the biblical experience with the unseen world is being constantly repeated today, and much of it in my own life, the significance and authority of scripture, especially the New Testament, is vastly increased for me.

And finally, some ground rules for finding one's way through the jungle of bookland without getting sidetracked, lost, or completely disgusted, may be to the point.

First, sample many books, writers and viewpoints. There is no merit in finishing every book that is started, or in starting any one that does not appeal by its style or viewpoint. Nor does it make sense to read material which is already familiar. Moreover, wide reading will keep one from being swept off one's feet by the first writer who deeply appeals to him. I have read some in at least half a dozen schools of oriental philosophy, and have learned from each while accepting none as having the last word. On the other hand, most of their devotees whom I know, are acquainted only with their favorite master or authority and are almost impervious to contrary ideas.

Secondly, read critically. Don't hesitate to question or doubt. If a book does not make sense to you, or does not appeal to you logically or aesthetically, don't try to make yourself swallow it regardless of the authority or friend who feels it is God's last and best word. Your taste is what counts, and your judgement and enjoyment are final for you. It is as true with reading as with eating, that one man's food is another man's poison.

Thirdly, read deeply. You will need to stretch both your intellectual and spiritual muscles if you are to grow. The greatest pleasure will often come from mastering a new idea after reading it five times. To understand the heights and depths of another man's experience is most rewarding whether one is ready to seek and accept it for himself or not. Nor will you be sure whether it is for your life if you do not know what is in his mind. This means you will sometimes get into deep water — over your head. But how else will you learn to swim, or find your way through the jungle?

Fourthly, respect the judgement of others, but do not be a slave to them. Because a book is a bestseller, it is a good idea for examining it, but it is not a good reason necessarily for either buying or reading it. Book lists should be suggestive, not compulsory. That applies also to the suggestions contained in this appendix. So because a book is not found in a recommended list, or is even subsidized or privately printed, do not therefore pass it by.

Lastly, borrow widely, but loan carefully. Many large libraries have more than you can ever read with profit, while the smaller ones can often get what you want from exchanges, and will sometimes buy good books which you suggest.

So have fun in the jungle, but don't get lost. You'll never be the same again.

Chapter Notes

ONE

1 *The Supreme Adventure* by Dr Robert Crookall; Clarke (Cambridge) 1961: pp. 119-122. *Intimations of Immortality* by Dr Robert Crookall; Clarke (Cambridge) 1965: pp. 23-29.

2 *Stranger Than Life* by DeWitt Miller; Ace (New York): pp. 156-160.

3 From *Fate* magazine, March 1967, p. 48.

TWO

1 See also *Eternal Life* by Harold Paul Sloan; Methodist (Philadelphia) 1948: pp. 51-53 (condensed).

2 From *Up the Golden Stair* by Elizabeth Yates; Dutton (New York) 1966.

3 From *The Answer is God* by Elise Miller Davis; p. 217.

4 In *The Luminous Trail* by Rufus Jones; p. 164.

5 *Search for Truth* by Ruth Montgomery; Morrow (New York) 1967: p. 243.

6 The best collections of those that are familiar to me are: *Death Bed Visions* by Sir William Barrett; (London) 1928 (Barrett was Professor of physics at the Royal College of Science in Ireland); and *One Hundred Cases for Survival After Death* by A. T. Baird, 1944.

7 *Deathbed Observations by Physicians and Nurses* by Dr Karlis Osis; Parapsychology Foundation (New York) 1961.

8 *The Last Crossing* by Gladys Osborne Leonard; (London) 1937: pp. 198-9.

9   *Fate* magazine, December 1967, pp. 87-8.

10   Quoted by Alson J. Smith from *Guideposts* in *Primer for the Perplexed;* Day (New York) 1962: p. 58. Also by DeWitt Miller in *You Take it With You* in *Coronet* magazine, April 1949.

11   In *Fate* magazine, September 1967.

12   See *Immortality — the Scientific Evidence* by Alson J. Smith; 1954: p. 27.

THREE

1   *On the Delay of Divine Justice* by Plutarch, quoted by G. R. S. Mead, F. W. H. Myers, Robert Crookall and others.

2   *Intimations of Immortality* by Dr Robert Crookall; Clarke (Cambridge) 1965.

3   *Human Personality and its Survival of Bodily Death,* by F. W. H. Myers; Longmans (New York) 1954: vol II p. 315 ff.

4   *op. cit.* p. 8 *Daily Sketch*, London, 14 October 1960.

5   *Clerical Errors* by Louis Tucker; Harper (New York) 1943; pp. 221 ff. (permission of Augusta Tucker).

6   In *How to make ESP Work for You* by Harold Sherman; DeVorss (Santa Monica) 1964: p. 131.

7   In *Breakthrough to Creativity* by Dr Shafica Karagulla; DeVorss (Santa Monica) 1967: pp. 121 ff.

8   *Deathbed Observations by Physicians and Nurses* by Dr Karlis Osis; Parapsychology Foundation (New York) 1961: pp. 30, 34 & 81.

9   By David Snell (senior editor) in *Life* magazine, 26 May 1967, p. 44.

FOUR

1   Quoted from *Eternal Life* by Dr Harold Paul Sloan; Methodist (Philadelphia) 1948: pp. 55 ff.

2   *Hidden Channels of the Mind* by Dr Louisa Rhine; Sloan (New York) 1961: p. 261.

3   *Human Personality and its Survival of Bodily Death,* by F. W. H. Myers; Longmans (New York) 1954: Vol II pp. 27-31.

4   From *The Resurrection and the Life* by Dr Leslie Weatherhead; Hodder (London), quoted by Raynor Johnson in *A Religious Outlook for Modern Man*; McGraw (New York) 1963: pp. 157-8.

5   From *The Transition Called Death* by Charles Hampton; Theosophical (Wheaton) 1943: pp. 19-20.

6   *How to Make ESP Work for You* by Harold Sherman; DeVorss (Santa Monica) 1964.

7   From *The Lighted Pathway* by Dr Frederick E. Chamberlain; (privately printed, Los Angeles, 1945): pp. 37-41.

FIVE

1   However, three recent books are: *The Enigma of Out-of-the-Body Travel* by Susy Smith; Helix (New York) 1965; *Journeys Out of the Body* by Robert Monroe (an American businessman who has learned to leave his almost at will), Doubleday (New York) 1971 and Souvenir (London) 1973; and *Life Without Death?* by Dr Nils O. Jacobson, Dell (New York) and Turnstone (London) 1974. In earlier works, Dr Crookall discusses almost 400 cases in two volumes, Sylvan Muldoon in three volumes, while Oliver Fox and Yram deal primarily with their personal experiences.

2   *The Twenty-Fifth Man* by Ed Morrell; New Era (Montclair) 1924: pp. 339-340.

3   Related by Susy Smith from Jung's *Memories, Dreams, Reflections*; Pantheon (New York) 1961 and Routledge & Collins (London) 1962.

4   *Breakthrough to Creativity* by Dr Shafica Karagulla; DeVorss (Santa Monica) 1967: pp. 72 & 73.

5   *The Night Side of Nature* by Catherine Crowe; Coates (Philadelphia) 1901: p. 217.

SIX

1   *Nothing So Strange* by Arthur Ford; Harper (New York) 1958.

2   *The Other Side* by Bishop James A. Pike; Doubleday (New York) 1968 & Allen (London) 1969.

3   *The American College Dictionary*; Random (New York) 1960.

SEVEN

1   *The Supreme Adventure* by Dr Robert Crookall; Clark (London) 1961, and several other works.

2   *The Unobstructed Universe* by Stewart Edward White; Dutton (New York) 1940.

3   *Many Lifetimes* by Denys Kelsey and Joan Grant; Doubleday (New York) 1967 and Gollancz (London) 1969: pp. 269 & 275.

4   *Deathbed Observations by Physicians and Nurses* by Dr Karlis Osis; Parapsychology Foundation (New York) 1961.

5   *The Road to Immortality* by Geraldine Cummins; Aquarian (London) 1932: p. 81.

6   *Livingstone the Liberator* by J. I. Macnair; Collins (London) 1969: p. 83.

7   *Unknown But Known* by Arthur Ford, p. 59. Also found in greater detail in his *Nothing so Strange*, pp. 160-2.

8   *The Supreme Adventure* by Dr Robert Crookall, p. 87.

9   *Deathbed Observations by Physicians and Nurses* by Dr Karlis Osis; Parapsychology Fndtn (New York) 1961: p. 29.

10 *The Transition Called Death* by Charles Hampton; Theosophical (Wheaton) 1943: p. 57.

11 *The Supreme Adventure* by Dr Robert Crookall, pp. 86-93.

12 *Intimations of Immortality* by Dr Robert Crookall; Clarke (London) 1965: pp. 12-13.

13 *The Road to Immortality* by Geraldine Cummins; Aquarian (London) 1932; p. 49.

14 *The Road to Immortality*, p. 87.

15 *Fate* magazine, May 1970.

16 *The Supreme Adventure* by Dr Robert Crookall, pp. 30-32.

EIGHT

1   *Arcana Coelestia*, n. 696.

2   *Heaven and Hell*, n. 574

3   *The Road to Immortality* by Geraldine Cummins; Aquarian (London) 1932: p. 49.

4   *Heaven and Hell*, n. 391.

5   *Gateway* (Monthly of the Spiritual Frontiers Fellowship, Evanston, edited by Laurence Heron), p. 209.

6   *A Religious Outlook for Modern Man* by Raynor Johnson; McGraw (New York) 1963: p. 173.

7   *Heaven and Hell,* n. 416.

8   *Conjugal Love,* nn. 68 & 321.

9   *Heaven and Hell,* n. 379.

10   *The Other Side* by Bishop James A. Pike; Doubleday (New York) 1968 & Allen (London) 1969.

11   *You Can Take it With You* by R. DeWitt Miller, p. 165.

12   *Travelers in Eternity* quoted by Raynor Johnson in *Nurselings of Immortality;* Harper (New York): p. 247.

13   *The Road to Immortality* by Geraldine Cummins; Aquarian (London) 1932: pp. 58-9.

14   *The Road to Immortality,* p. 39.

NINE

1   *Arcana Coelestia,* n. 696.

2   *Heaven and Hell,* n. 574.

3   *The Road to Immortality,* pp. 47-9.

4   *The Going and the Glory* by Gloria Lee. (Given through a medium "Verity" of Auckland, published in New Zealand)

5   *The Road to Immortality,* p. 39.

6   *Beyond Human Personality,* by Frederic Myers, p. 38.

TEN

1   *Spiritual Frontiers,* (Quarterly of Spiritual Frontiers Fellowship, Volume one.

2   *Man and His Universe* by Langdon-Davies, quoted by Sir Alister Hardy.

3   *From Mystery to Meaning,* Matson, Pageant (New York) 1955.

ELEVEN

1   Published as *Immortality of the Soul or Resurrection of the Dead;* Epworth (London) 1958.

2   *Heaven and Hell* by John Sutherland Bonnell; Abingdon (Nashville) 1956: p. 35.